Horatio Gor

Moko; or Maori Tattooing

Elibron Classics
www.elibron.com

Elibron Classics series.

ISBN 1-4212-6911-2 (paperback)
ISBN 1-4212-6910-4 (hardcover)

This Elibron Classics Replica Edition is an unabridged facsimile of the edition published in 1896 by Chapman & Hall, Ltd., London.

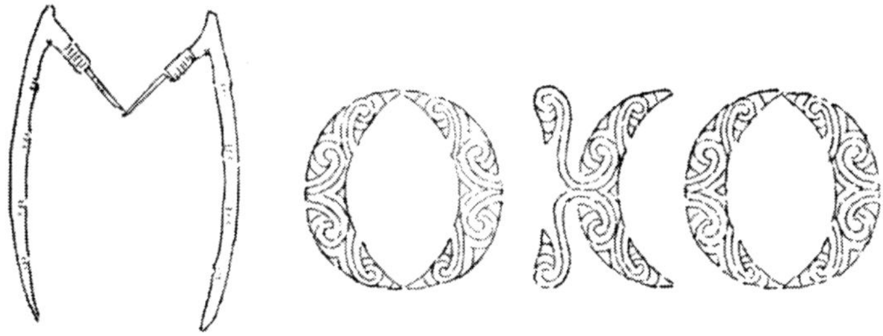

The M consists of Tattooing Instruments. The remaining Letters are made up of scrolls from moko.

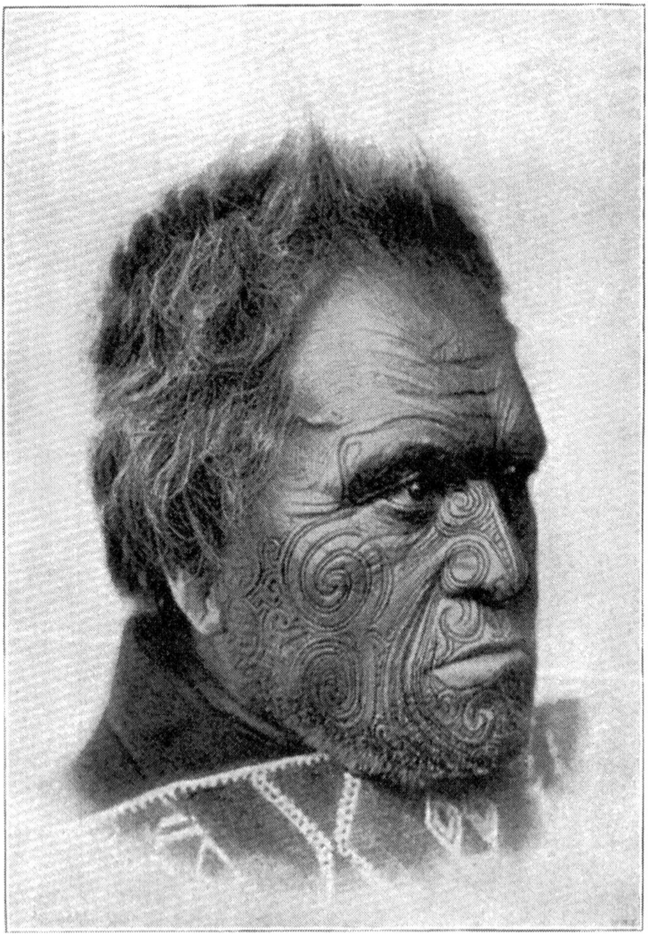

A Chief's Tattooing.

MOKO; OR

MAORI TATTOOING

BY

MAJOR-GENERAL ROBLEY

WITH 180 ILLUSTRATIONS FROM DRAWINGS BY THE AUTHOR AND FROM PHOTOGRAPHS

LONDON: CHAPMAN AND HALL, LIMITED

1896

Richard Clay and Sons, Limited,
LONDON AND BUNGAY.

TO

THOSE WHO HAVE SERVED AGAINST

WARRIORS OF NEW ZEALAND

I Dedicate

THIS LITTLE BOOK

H. G. R.

PREFACE

My main object in this book is to present a series of illustrations of the art of moko or tattooing, as practised by the Maoris. It is fast vanishing, and a record of it by one who has studied the subject for many years may be worth publication. I have learnt all I could of moko in New Zealand, and from the best sources; and such skill as I have as an artist has long been employed in setting down my notes in the form of drawings. Literary skill I cannot claim; but I have collected all I can get in the way of information from numerous authorities, a list of which is appended. My personal experiences during the Maori campaign of 1864–66 and my subsequent inquiries have enabled me to form and express some opinions of my own and to add a little independent matter. But I wish to express my indebtedness to very many writers whose works I have laid under contribution. It is, however, as a means of publishing my drawings, sketches, and photographs that I have put my notes together in the form they now take.

The beautiful arabesques in moko patterns might, I think,

commend themselves to art students and designers, as well as to students of ethnology and folk lore; for the native artist in moko must be entitled to the credit of great originality and taste in his patterns; and his skill was such as to class him among the world's artists. These designs seem to me to contain a mine of wealth to the modern student.

I have to express my sincere gratitude to many respected friends and acquaintances for kind assistance. I am most indebted to many polite strangers in all parts of the world, curators of museums, and others, upon whom I have intruded, and who have courteously responded to my inquiries and to my appeals for help; and the number of these obligations is so large that I can only make this general acknowledgment of them. In conclusion, I wish again to say that I hope my book will be judged of by the illustrations and not by the letterpress. I began to collect my pictures long ago, when the art of moko was a living one. It is now in a state of decay, and my hope is that such little skill as I have in depicting the old art of moko will be appreciated by those who sympathise with art in whatever form it is presented.

TWO LETTERS.

THE RIGHT HON. SIR GEORGE GREY, K.C.B., TO THE AUTHOR.

7 PARK PLACE,
ST. JAMES'S, S.W.
3rd August, 1894.

DEAR SIR,—I think your illustrations of Maori tattooing are interesting and valuable, as they give with great correctness some of the patterns of Maori tattooing; and the portraits are equally interesting as they give excellent illustrations of the art of "moko" which is rapidly passing away, and will soon be forgotten.

Faithfully yours,
G. GREY

THE RIGHT HON. SIR JOHN LUBBOCK, BART., M.P., TO THE AUTHOR.

HIGH ELMS,
FARNBOROUGH, R.S.O.
1st December, 1894.

DEAR SIR,—I beg to acknowledge the receipt of your letter, and shall be happy to see your book on New Zealand tattooing.

It is most important to preserve all evidence of a life which is rapidly disappearing.

I am, yours truly,
JOHN LUBBOCK.

CONTENTS

PART I.—MOKO

PART II.—MOKOMOKAI

ILLUSTRATIONS

PART I

MOKO

MOKO AND MOKOMOKAI

CHAPTER I

HOW MOKO FIRST BECAME KNOWN TO EUROPEANS

History may yet have more to tell us about the Maoris, but the earliest record of them we have is in the journal of the celebrated traveller Abel Tasman. His visit to New Zealand in December, 1642, was very short, and it ended in bloodshed. But Tasman and the artist who accompanied him, though they record much of the personal appearance of the Maori, make no mention of tattooing. We can hardly suppose that this remarkable feature escaped their observation, since the figure, complexion, hair, and dress are all described; and the conclusion is that in Tasman's days moko or tattooing did not exist. The Maori has only legends and oral traditions to account for his presence in New Zealand and for his customs such as moko. Maori tradition sheds little light on the origin of this custom. There is no reference in song or chant to help the investigator; and the most that can be done is to compare the observations of navigators with the latest knowledge. In this way we learn something of its rudiments, of its early simplicity, of its later richness and more perfect design, and ultimately of its decay. After a long gap of one hundred and twenty-seven years, we come upon the next mention of the Maori in history; and during that space of time nothing is known of New Zealand. Not until Captain Cook, the great navigator, visited these Islands in 1769 was anything more known. Captain Cook and the *Endeavour* returned to England in June, 1771, and then it was that the subject of this book became known. The treasures he brought back from the Southern Hemisphere and the drawings and journals he made will be referred to presently. In his time moko was much used in New Zealand. Native tradition has it that their first settlers used to mark their faces for battle with charcoal, and that the lines on the face thus made were the beginnings of the tattoo. To save the trouble of this constantly painting their warlike decorations on the face, the lines were made permanent. Hence arose the practice of carving the face, and the body with dyed incisions. The Reverend Mr. Taylor (an accepted authority on matters relating to the natives of New Zealand) is of opinion that moko or tattooing originated otherwise; and he assumes that the chiefs being of a lighter race and having to fight side by side with slaves of darker hues darkened their faces in order to appear of the same race. These two methods of accounting for the origin of moko are not inconsistent, and both may have had their share in bringing about the results which it is proposed to consider. No reliable evidence whatever exists as to the nature, meaning, extent, or elaboration of primitive moko. But the fact need not diminish its interest.

The term tattoo is not known in New Zealand; and the name given to the decorative marks in question, though elsewhere so called, is in New Zealand moko. The subject, it is true, exercised almost a fascination for the great navigator Captain Cook, who practically rediscovered New Zealand after it had first been visited (as already narrated) in 1642 by Tasman; and to Captain Cook we owe the first full and faithful description of moko, for he gave to it the full force of his unrivalled powers of observation. So important are his comments and notes on the subject that I shall refer to them at some length in the course of this chapter. For the moment I will digress to deal with early historical mention of markings of this nature. Herodotus appears to refer to it as being customary among the Thracians, where he says: "To have punctures on their skin is with them a mark of nobility; to be without these is a testimony of mean descent." This remark suggests a curious analogy between the ancient Thracian noble and the modern Maori chief. Plutarch says that the Thracians of his time made tattoo marks on their wives to avenge the death of Orpheus whom they had murdered in Mœnad fury while celebrating the mysteries of Bacchus. And it is not a little remarkable that a custom should be at one time a punishment to the female sex, when it was or had been an ornament to the other.

There are other references to the custom, and these all tend to show how widely diffused it was. It is, for instance, evidently alluded to (together with the practice of wounding the body to show mourning) in Leviticus (chap. xix). At the twenty-eighth verse we read: "Ye shall not make any cuttings in your flesh for the dead, nor *print any marks* upon you." It is reasonable to suppose that both injunctions were directed against a practice common amongst neighbouring nations, which the chosen people according to their usual propensity showed a tendency to imitate. Pliny too states that the dye with which the Britons stained themselves was that of a herb *glastum*; that they introduced the juice with punctures previously made in the skin so as to form permanent delineations of various animals and other objects.

I will now deal with Captain Cook's remarks.

On Sunday, October 8th, 1769, Captain Cook records that the first native with moko was shot, and notes that one side of the face was tattooed in spiral lines of a regular pattern. The navigator calls the tattooing "amoco." In recounting his first voyage, Captain Cook says each separate tribe seemed to have a different custom in regard to tattooing; for those in some canoes seemed to be covered with the marking; while those in other canoes showed scarcely a stain except on the lips, which were black in all cases. He says: "The bodies and faces are marked with black stains they call amoco—broad spirals on each buttock—the thighs of many were almost entirely black, the faces of the old men are almost covered. By adding to the tattooing they grow old and honourable at the same time."

And again: "The marks in general are spirals drawn with great nicety and even elegance. One side corresponds with the other. The marks in the body resemble the foliage in old chased ornaments, convolutions of filigree work, but in these they have such a luxury of forms that of a hundred which at first appeared exactly the same no two were formed alike on close examination."

And in the course of his first voyage he describes some of the New Zealanders as having their thighs stained entirely black, with the exception only of a few narrow lines, "so that at first

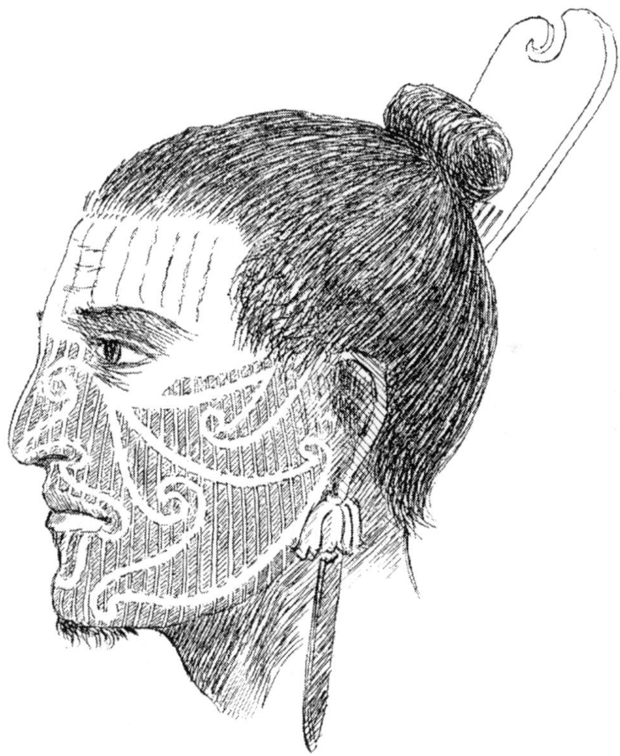

Fig. 1.—From an original drawing for Captain Cook's Voyages.
(*British Museum, Additional Manuscripts Room.*)

sight they appeared to wear striped breeches." He observes that the quantity and form of these marks differ widely in different parts of the coast and islands; and that the older men appeared to be more profusely decorated. One may almost regret that a practice which suited the Maoris and which involves so much art and skill is rapidly dying out under modern influences. In Captain Cook's time it was very generally practised and was carried to a point of ferocious perfection which never failed to

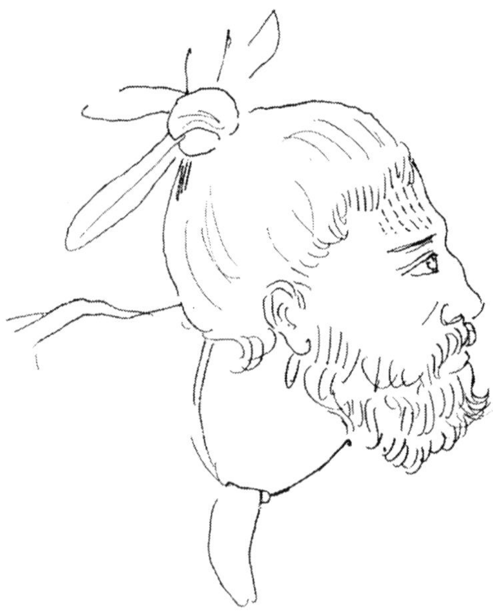

FIG. 2.—From one of Sydney Parkinson's drawings. One of the earliest known and incomplete patterns.

attract the visitor who regained his ship. With Captain Cook was Sydney Parkinson, the clever draughtsman employed by Mr. Joseph Banks; and Parkinson's journal gives some account of moko as it was in 1769, besides the first drawings of it. He says: "As to the tattowing, it is done very curiously in spiral

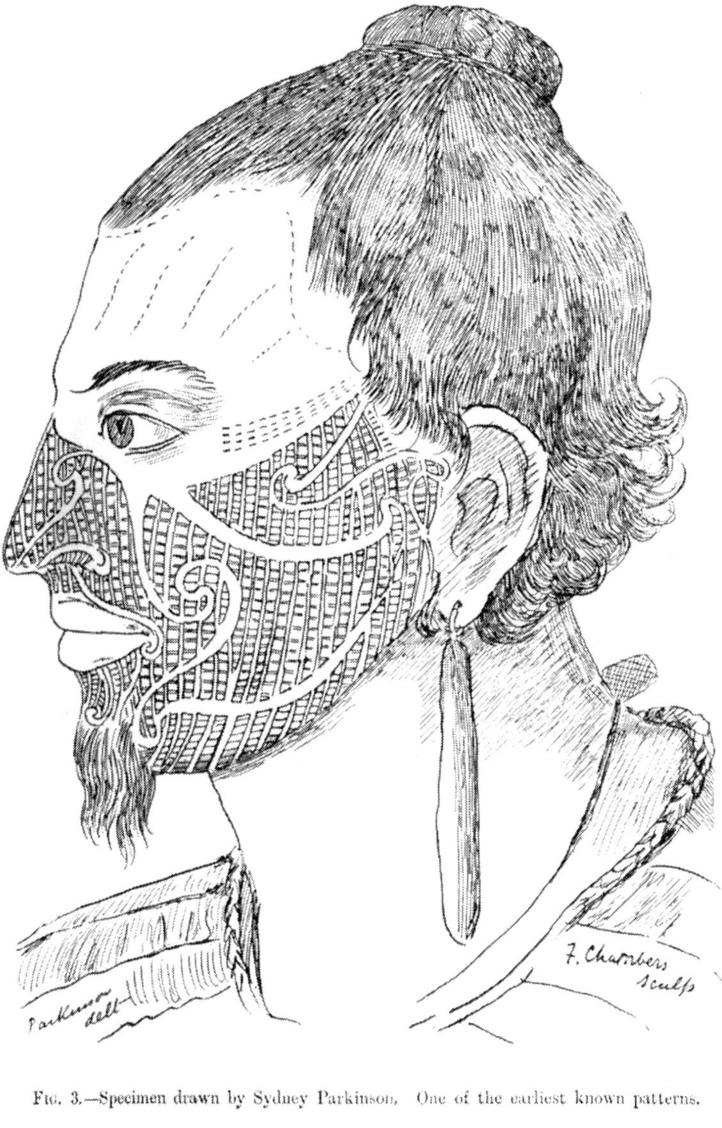

FIG. 3.—Specimen drawn by Sydney Parkinson. One of the earliest known patterns.

and other figures; and in many places indented into their skins which looks like carving, though at a distance it appears as if it had been only smeared with a black paint."

And he adds: "The tattowing is peculiar to the principal men among them."

Also at another part of the coast, he says: "These people were much like them we had seen heretofore; excepting that they were more tattowed: most of them had the figures of volutes on their lips, and several had their thighs and part of their bellies marked."

"The tattow on their faces was not done in spirals, but in different figures from what we had ever seen before."

His account of the tattooing of the women I shall refer to in my chapter devoted to that part of the subject. A great authority, Mr. W. Colenso of Napier, says of Parkinson's portrait of a chief, that it bears a style of tattooing which has long become extinct and of which he only saw a few specimens some 40 years ago. Three of Parkinson's sketches of Maoris tattooed in the style of 1770 or thereabouts are given in my illustrations.

In the Additional Manuscripts Room, British Museum, are many of the original drawings in pencil and colour taken during Cook's voyages.

Subsequently to Captain Cook's visits to the New Zealand islands, several early navigators, travellers, and missionaries have published their observations on the subject of moko, and mention should be made of the works of Mr. Savage and Mr. Nicholas, who were among these earlier visitors. The periodical reports of the Church Missionary Society also have frequently treated of this

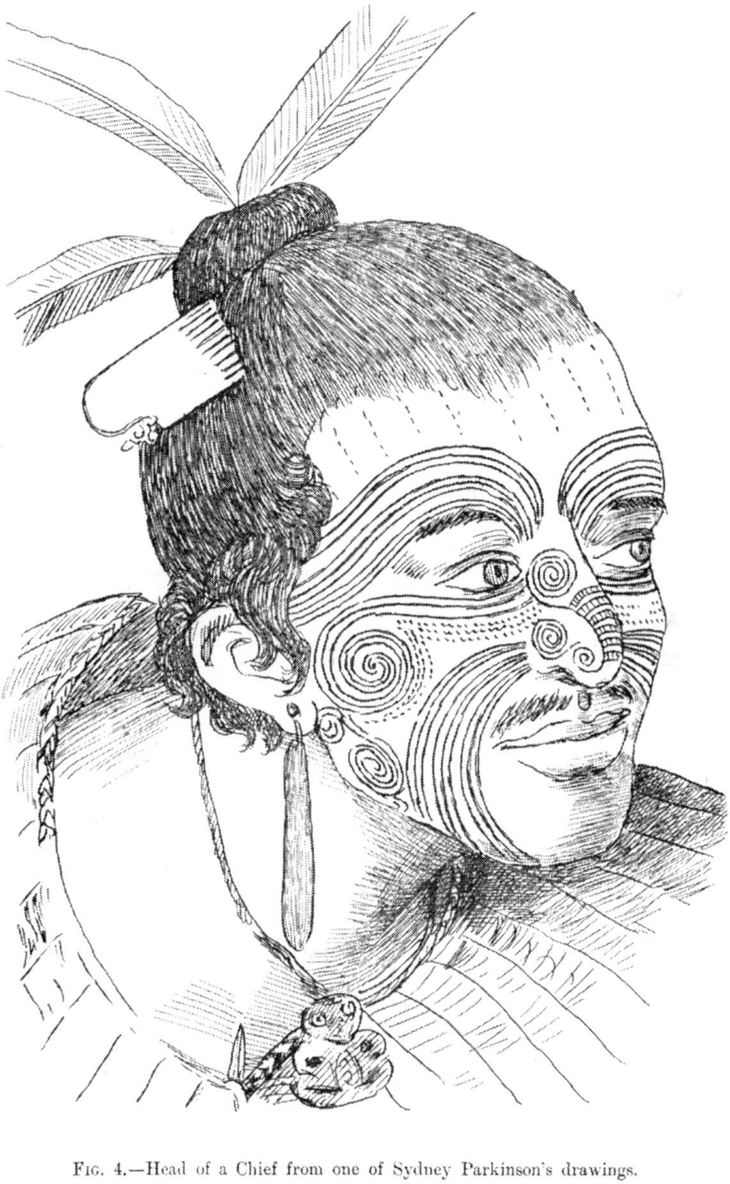

Fig. 4.—Head of a Chief from one of Sydney Parkinson's drawings.

national decoration. I must also refer to the reports of Crozet's voyages in 1771-2, of which mention will again be made.

While speaking of the tattooing practised with so much art and skill by the Maoris and other inhabitants of Polynesia, I must quote Sir John Lubbock's valuable opinion. Speaking of Polynesian tattooing, he says that perhaps the most beautiful of all was that of the New Zealanders who were tattooed in spiral lines. The process, he adds, is extremely painful, particularly on the lips, but to shrink from it or even to show any signs of suffering while undergoing the operation was considered unmanly.

The mode of tattooing practised by the Maoris was unlike that of any other race, and their artistic designs were so arranged that the skin of the face was often completely covered up to the corners

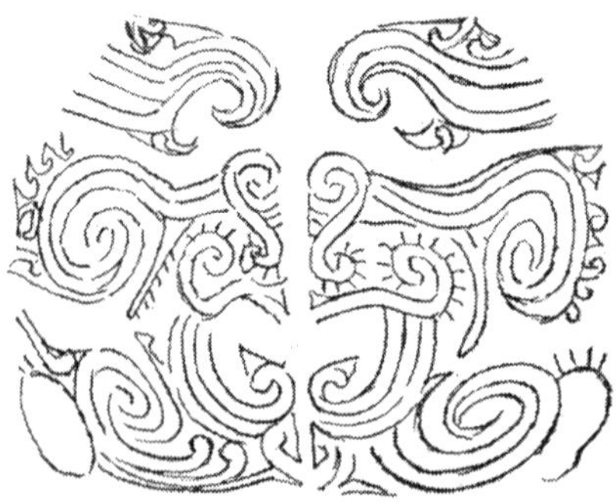

FIG. 5.—Specimen of a Moko signature.

of the eyes, and even over the eyelids; and that the stains, though tending to diminish in brilliancy, were indelible. But doubtful as the meaning of moko is, there were uses for it. Some portion of it, some distinctive part, was a mark of identity, and has been copied for Europeans by the Maoris as a signature. For instance, Mr. Wakefield records that in a purchase of land near the Bay of Islands by Mr. Samuel Marsden, the famous missionary, in place of signatures to the deed, facsimiles of the face-moko of the vendors were drawn on the document. This was in 1815. The deeds were witnessed by Messrs. Kendal and Nicholson on the part of the

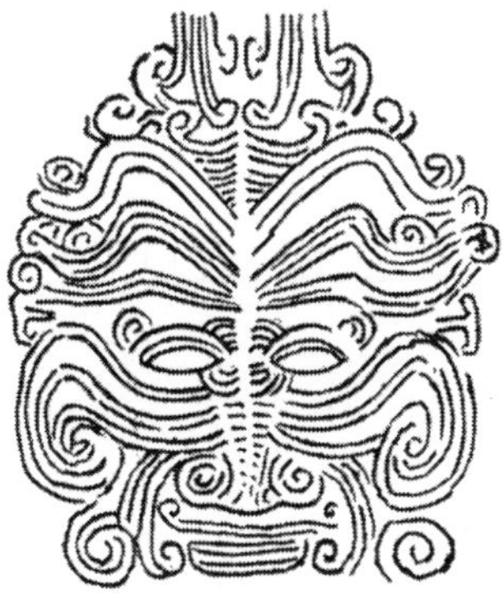

FIG. 6.—A Moko signature.
Kowiti, Chief of Waimate and Maunganui.

purchasers, and on the part of the vendors by a native carpenter who drew the moko of one of his cheeks in place of a signature. The same writer mentions that the deeds and copies which conveyed the plains of Wairau (in consideration of a ship's gun) were signed with elaborate drawings of the face-moko of the chiefs. Letourneau notices a similar practice which may, in fact, be compared to the use of a seal in our country. Polack, too, speaks of the pride the New Zealanders take in adding the various curvatures of the moko to their signatures: "Our risibility has," he says, "often been excited in viewing an aged chief, whose scant locks have weathered upwards of seventy winters, drawing with intense care his signature, with inclined head and extended tongue, as is the wont of young European practitioners in the art of penmanship."

These moko signatures give some interesting history and designs. Here is a curious autograph sketch of the face-moko

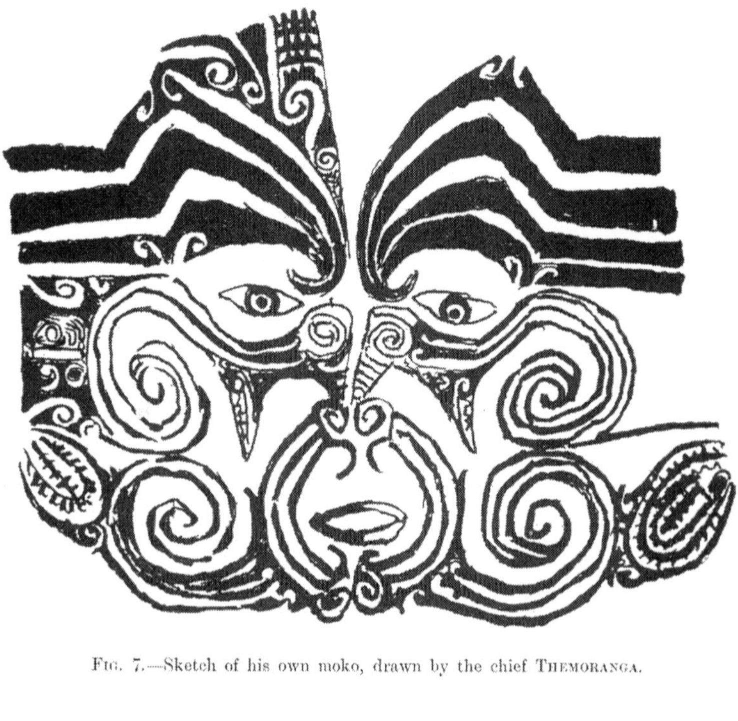

FIG. 7.—Sketch of his own moko, drawn by the chief THEMORANGA.

of a chief named Themoranga, as drawn by himself with a pen—an instrument which he handled on that occasion for the first time in his life. It is dated 9th March, 1815, and was done on board the *Active*. It shows a face of elaborate moko still

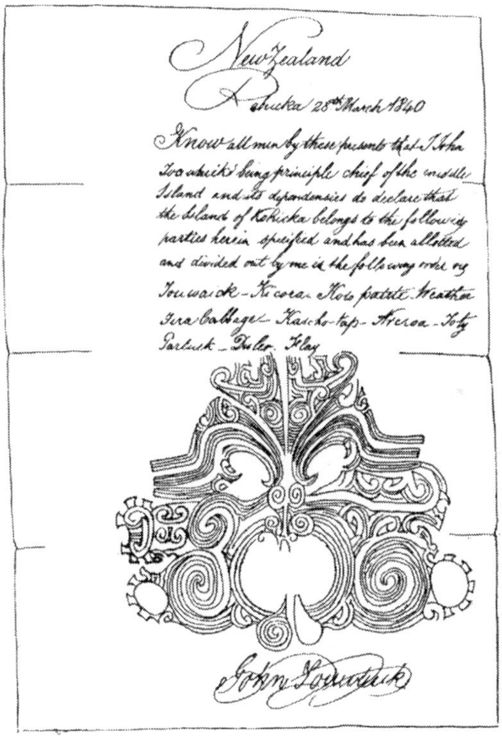

FIG. 8.—Moko signature on a deed.

(*The original in the possession of* DR. HOCKEN, *of Dunedin, N.Z.*

This is a land grant signed by TUAWHAIKI (*alias* "Bloody Jack"), a chief of Otago (Ngaitahu tribe). He was a great enemy of Rauparaha, who signed the Wairau deeds.

incomplete; the left half of the lips, the left cheek, the left upper forehead, are unfinished. Another remarkable work of art is a drawing of himself by Te Pehi Kupe, a fine piece of moko which must be taken as correct. His body was also plentifully covered with marks; and his fine muscular arms were

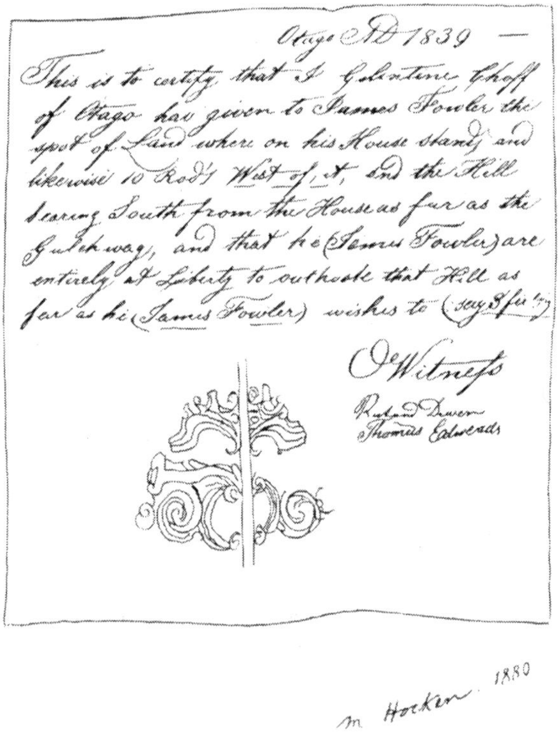
Otago Nov 1839 —
This is to certify that I Golontine Chief of Otago hav given to James Fowler the spot of Land where on his House stands and likewise 10 Rod's West of it, and the Hill bearing South from the House as far as the Gutchway, and that he (James Fowler) are entirely at Liberty to outhoole that Hill as far as he (James Fowler) wishes to (say 8 feet)
Witness
Richard Dawson
Thomas Edwards

M Hocken 1880

Fig. 9.—Moko signature on a deed.
(*The original in the possession of* Dr. Hocken, *of Dunedin, N.Z.*)
This is a land grant by the chief Golontine Korako.

in particular furrowed by numerous single black lines, which he said denoted the number of wounds he had received in battle.

Te Pehi Kupe (whose daughter had been killed and cooked)

was in England in 1826 to procure arms to revenge the onslaughts of the northern tribes. He gave some valuable information on the subject of moko when sitting for his portrait, for he was very anxious that the marks on his face should be accurately copied. One mark just over his nose was, he said, his name—"Europee man write with pen his name—Te Pehi's is here" (pointing to his forehead); and he delineated on paper the

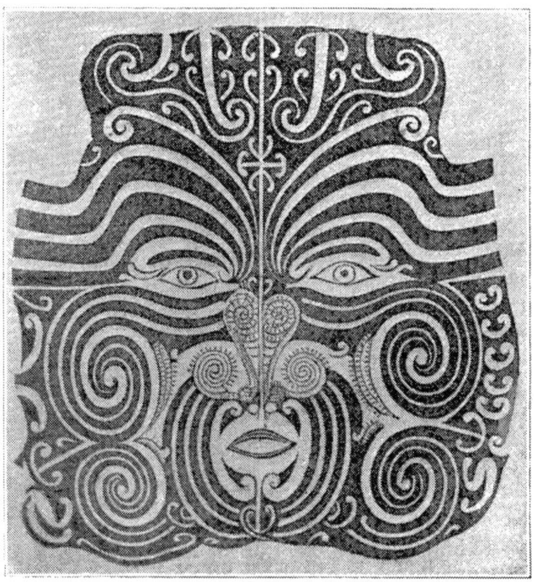

FIG. 10.—Tattooing on the face of TE PEHI KUPE, drawn by himself.

corresponding marks or names of his brother and of his son. Every line, both on his face and on other parts of his body, was firmly registered on his memory. The portrait of his moko was drawn by him without the aid of a mirror. During his stay in Liverpool he was besieged with applications for specimens of his art, and for a fortnight a large part of his time was occupied in turning out sketches of his face. The depth and profusion of the moko, he said, indicated the dignity of the individual; and little of the original surface of his face remained. Some of his sketches represented moko on other portions of his body. He drew for Dr. Traill the mokos of his brother and of his son; and on finishing the latter, he held it up and gazed on it with a murmur of affectionate delight, kissing it many times and, as he presented it, burst into tears.

Te Pehi's statement that the more elaborate the moko the higher was the rank implied may have been true, but it was by no means the case always among the Maoris. The time he had for the artists, the wishes and power of endurance of the patient, had no doubt much to do with the nature and extent of the pattern. Many of the great chiefs were only partly decorated; and the likeness of the king who was a visitor here in 1884 accompanied by four chiefs will show that even King Tawhiao was far behind Te Pehi in elaborate decoration. It must be admitted that a man with such a pattern drawn on his face as Te Pehi had was entitled to assume the *rôle* of a critic on tattooing.[1]

[1] Te Pehi failed to obtain the firearms which had made Hongi so successful a warrior. He returned home and was with a number of his friends killed and eaten by a Middle Island tribe, amongst whom he rashly trusted himself. In revenge, an expedition was arranged in 1830; and Captain Stewart of the brig *Elizabeth*, an Englishman, lent his aid to the revolting scenes which ensued. On the promise of a cargo of flax, he sailed with a war party on board, and entered into communication with the enemy, enticed the enemy's chief on board and

I am anxious to give the reader all that the best authorities have told us on the subject of moko, and will here add D'Urville's

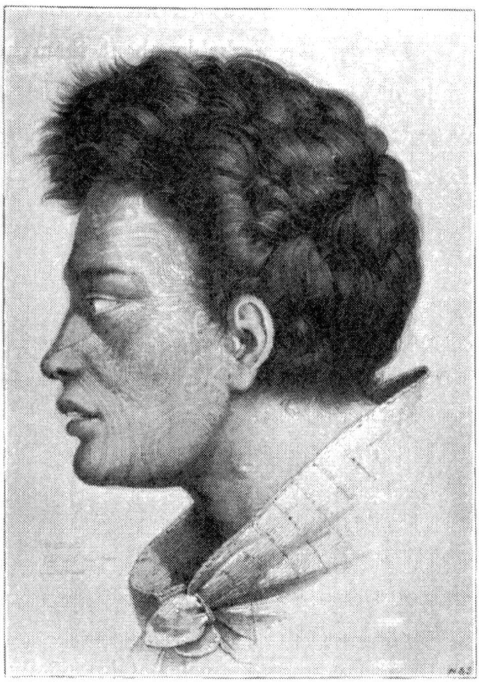

FIG. 11.—From a drawing in Dumont D'Urville's Voyages.

views. He professes to see in Maori moko a complete analogy to European heraldry, but with this difference—that whereas the

lulled his followers into a false idea of security. Captain Stewart's friends then massacred the tribe, and brought 500 baskets of human flesh and 50 prisoners on board his vessel where the ship's coppers were used to prepare the cannibal feast. Stewart on returning failed to obtain payment for these services. He arrived at Sydney January 14th, 1831, where a captain of some vessel had carried the news coat-of-arms attests the merits of ancestors, the Maori moko illustrates the merits of the person decorated with it.

He says: "Tuai one day was calling my attention with great pride to some curious designs cut on his forehead, and when I asked him what there was remarkable about them he answered: 'Only the family of Coro-coro in the whole of New Zealand has the right to bear these signs. Congui, most powerful as he is, could not adopt them, for the family of Coro-coro is much more

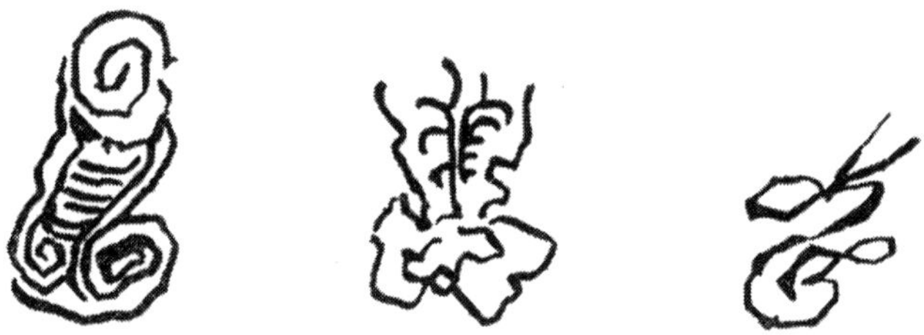

HARA. WAKATERI. TITORE.

FIG. 12.—Signatures of chiefs of the Bay of Islands. (c. 1830—1835.)

illustrious than his.' A New Zealander one day examining the seal of an English officer noticed the arms engraved on it and asked him if the design was the moko of his family."

But Mr. Tregear states: "I do not think there is any mark distinguishing tribes, still we do not know everything (probably never will know) about the full significance of tattau."

It has been used as a method of communication, and the Rev.

and where he was shunned, and then was tried, but evidence being out of the way he escaped. Though human vengeance did not reach him, he dropped dead on the deck of the *Elizabeth* while rounding Cape Horn, and his body reeking with rum was pitched overboard by his crew with little ceremony and no regret.

Mr. Taylor says: "The Maori used a kind of hieroglyphic or symbolical way of communication. Thus a chief inviting another to join in a war party sent a tattooed potato and a fig of tobacco bound up together; which was interpreted to mean by the tattoo that the enemy was a Maori, and not European, and by the tobacco that it represented smoke; the other chief, on receiving the missive, roasted the one (the potato) and ate it, and smoked the other (the tobacco) to show he accepted the invitation and would join him with his guns and powder."

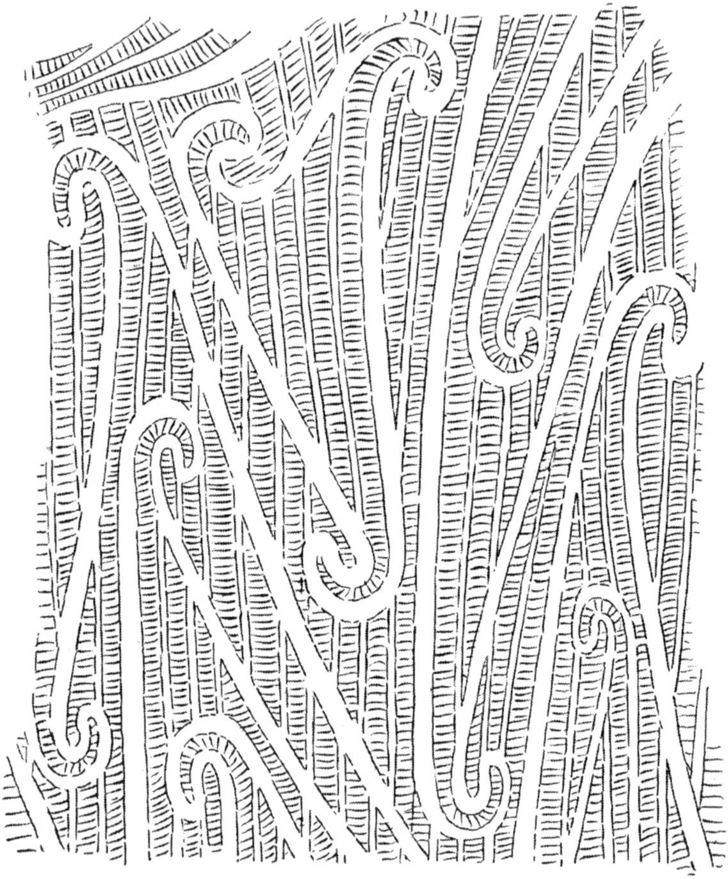

FIG. 13.—Tracing from a thigh-skin in the possession of the Author.
(Reduced to two-thirds of life size.)

CHAPTER II

MOKO MEN

SOME reference has already been made to the uncertainty attaching to the object with which moko was practised by the men of the Maori race; but some further speculations on this

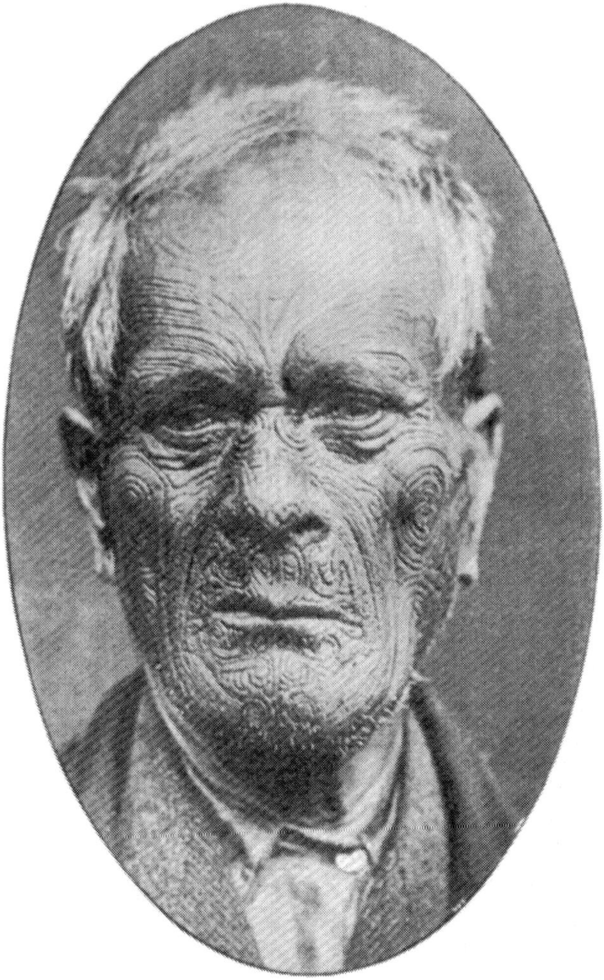

Fig. 14.—A well-chiselled head, with deep incision.

subject suggest themselves. Not only to become more terrible in war, when fighting was carried on at close quarters, but to

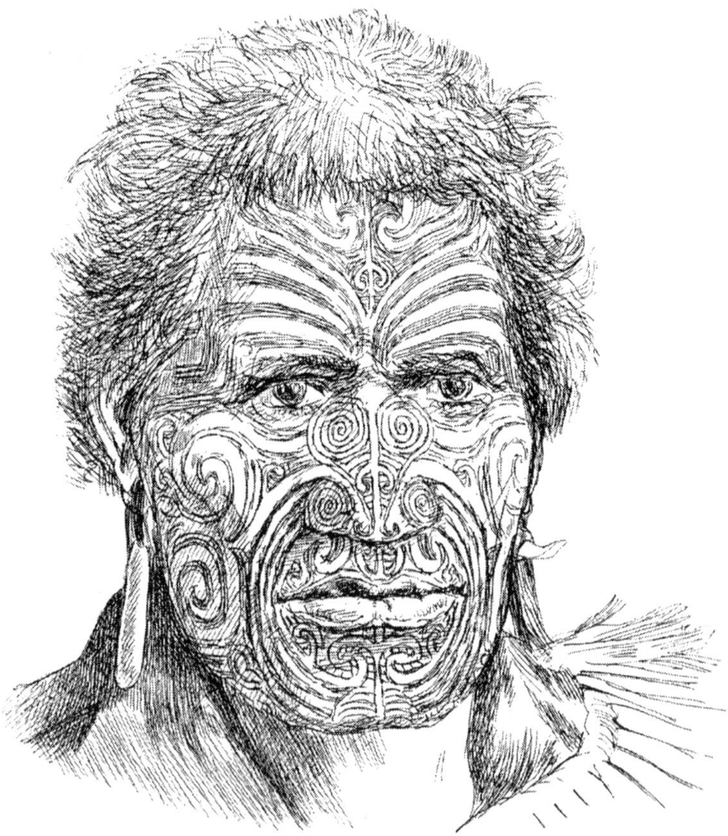

Fig. 15.—From life by the Author, showing good nose-marking.

appear more distinguished and attractive to the female sex, must certainly be included. The great chiefs had their faces and bodies covered with designs of extreme delicacy and beauty; and all the men, except the slaves, were more or less decorated with blue-black; and the fact that slaves were excluded from the art is significant of the views of their masters. It has been said that the tattooing on the bodies was for the purpose of identification in case the head was cut off by the enemy in battle. Moko was a

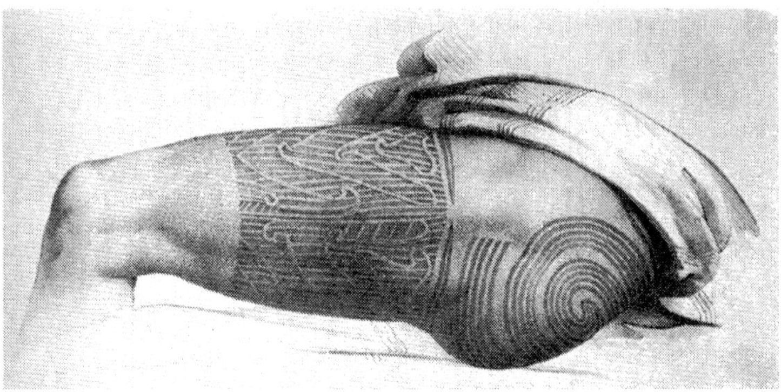

FIG. 16.—Thigh-tattooing.
(*From Dumont D'Urville's "Voyages."*)

sign of distinction; it told off the noble and freeman from the slave.

Maning, a famous writer on old Maori life before the remembrance of it had quite passed away, thus describes a war party: "As I have said, the men were all stripped for action, but I also notice that the appearance of nakedness is completely taken away by the tattooing, the colour of the skin, and the arms and equipments. . . . The men, in fact, look much better than when dressed in their Maori clothing. Every man almost without exception is covered with tattooing from the knees to the waist; the face is also covered with dark spiral lines."

Mr. Edward Tregear remarks that the tattooing of a slave's face was only a vile practice introduced for the horrible purpose of selling the dried head.

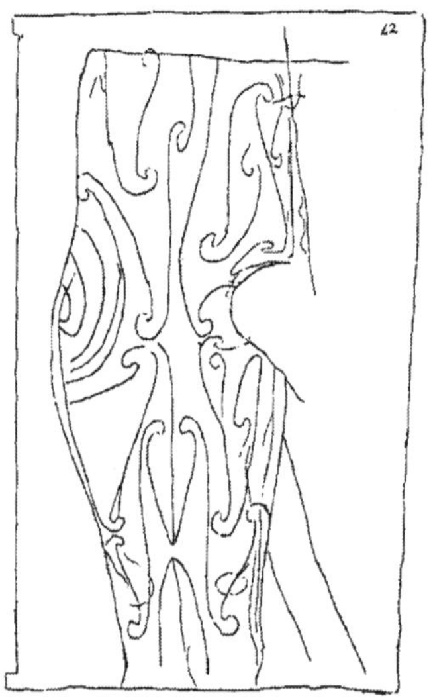

FIG. 17.—Body-tattooing.

(From original drawing for Captain Cook's "Voyages," in the British Museum, Additional Manuscripts Room.)

In 1814 the first three native magistrates were appointed, and being chiefs were also "men of mark."

Rutherford, whom I shall have other occasion to mention, states that in the part of the country where he was detained in captivity in 1816 the men were usually tattooed on the face, hips, and body, sometimes as low down as the knee; but that none were allowed to be decorated on the forehead, upper lip, and chin, except the

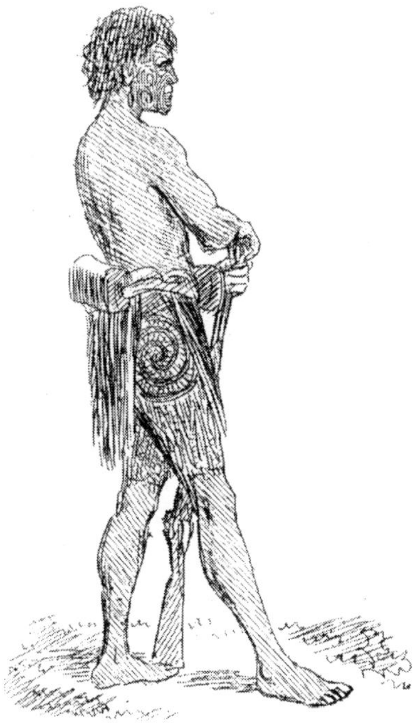

Fig. 18.—Thigh-tattooing.

great ones of the tribe. Priests, it seems, were either exempt or forbidden the tattoo.

Mr. Wakefield expressly states that this was so with regard to the *tangata tapu*, or sacred personages; and Mr. Savage (1807) records that the pantaloons are in general very highly embroidered, of which they are not a little vain; and that the *tohungas*, or priests, had only a small patch of moko over the right eye.

Of course it was a source of pride to the owner, and in Crozet's voyages (1771–72) it is stated that there were marks on the hands, and noted that the chiefs were very pleased to show the tattooing

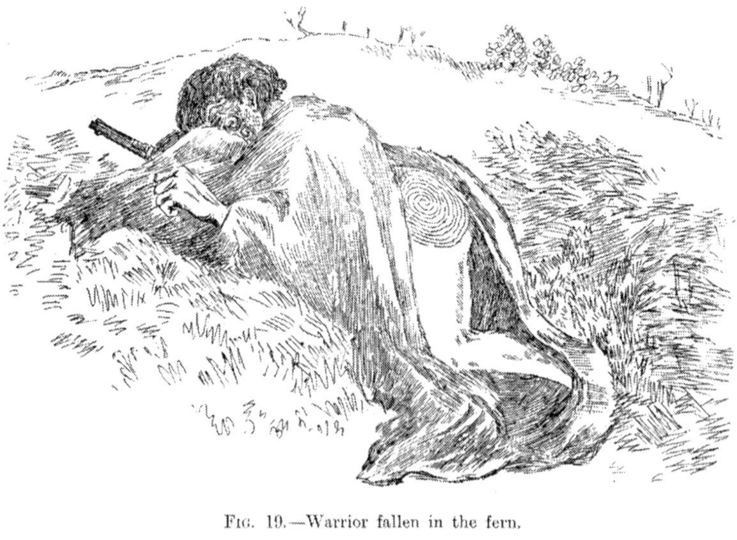

Fig. 19.—Warrior fallen in the fern.
(*From a drawing by the Author*, 1864.)

on their bodies. He notes that the moko on the faces was very diverse, but that on the buttocks it always seems to be the same—a neat spiral line, of which the first or starting point is at the centre of the most fleshy part, then successively embraces the whole circumferences. To have fine tattooed faces was the great ambition among men both to render themselves attractive to the ladies and conspicuous in war. The decorative art of a people reflects their character; and the fierceness of the Maori moko undoubtedly corresponded to fierceness in their nature. For even if killed by the enemy, whilst the heads of the untattooed were treated with indignity and kicked on one side, those which were conspicuous by their beautiful moko were carefully cut off—stuck

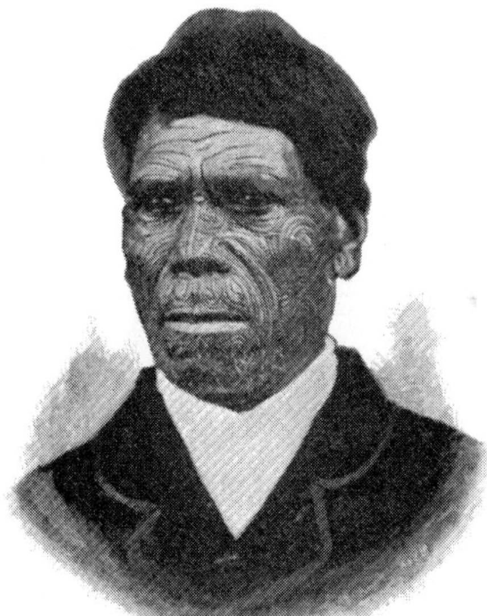

Fig. 20.—A Native Preacher.

on the *turuturu*, a pole with a cross on it, and preserved; all of which was highly gratifying to the survivors, and the spirits of their late possessor. One sketch depicts this practice.

To set off moko to advantage it was necessary to give up all idea of a beard and the wearing of hair on the face which was not considered in the light of an ornament. Consequently it was necessary for the men to submit to the pain of pulling out the hair by the roots. The great object of chiefs was to excite fear amongst their enemies by every possible means—the doing so almost insured

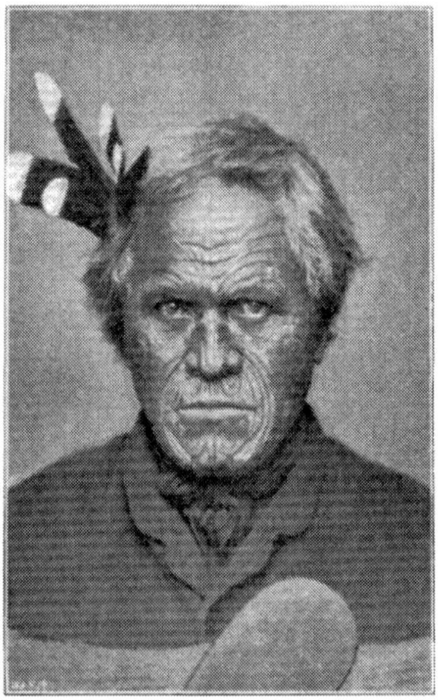

FIG. 21.—A Chief's tattooing: a full face of the portrait given as frontispiece.

success. He rendered his countenance as terrible as possible in the older days with charcoal and red ochre; the face being marked with lines of the former, and the head and person smeared over with the latter. And to give him a permanent dignity the tattoo was invented.

The deep tortuous lines of moko add fierceness to features strongly marked, and give hardness and rigour to those muscles which are acted upon by the softer passions.

In former days a pair of mussel shells were employed, but since the acquaintance with Europeans large tweezers have taken their place, and were generally hanging from the garment or neck; and whenever the gentleman could find no other employment he indefatigably occupied himself with them.

To allow the beard to grow was regarded as a sign of old age and proof that the wearer had ceased to care for his appearance; a person with a beard was addressed as E weki, which is a salutation equivalent to old man. "But this," says the Rev. Mr. Taylor, a missionary in New Zealand for more than thirty years (his book printed 1870), "is no longer the case; since the

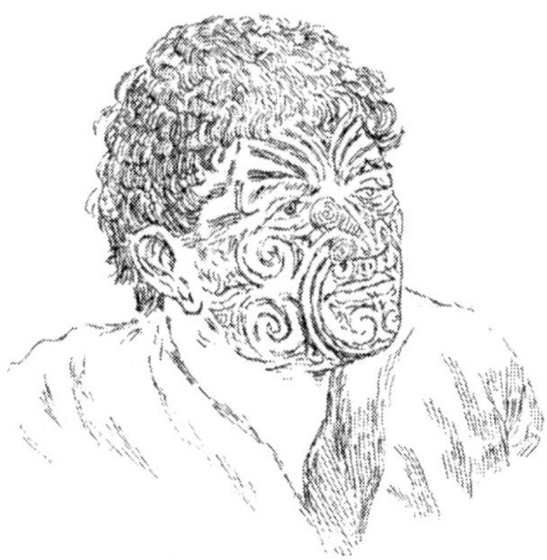

FIG. 22.—A young Chief fully tattooed, bayoneted in left eyebrow.
(*From a drawing by the Author*, 1864.)

tattoo was given up the beard has been adopted in its place, and that of the natives rivals the most luxuriant one of the Europeans."

That the face should be unmarked with moko rendered a man

liable to the term "Papatea," or plain-face; anyhow he looked a *tutua*, or poor nobody. It will be seen that the New

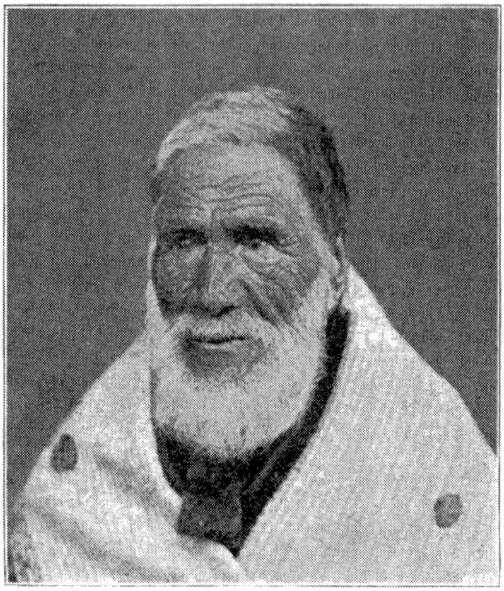

Fig. 23.—An aged Chief wearing hair over moko.

Zealanders attached to the word "plain" a meaning in relation to human appearance far more literal than the use of the term by Europeans.

In 1864-66, when staying in the delightful New Zealand country, I took several sketches of natives showing moko on the face covered with hair, for though the practice of moko was then fairly vigorous, yet the growth of beard and moustache was common among the natives, with the exception of the older men. The older men being well tattooed never used to wear hair on the face.

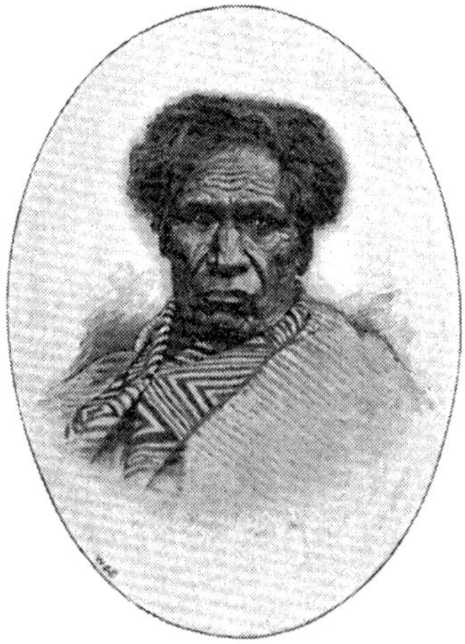

FIG. 24.—Type of Maori.

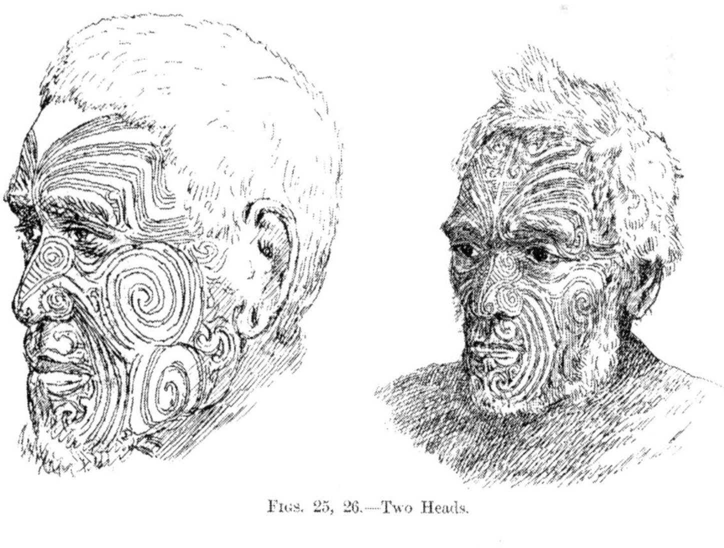

FIGS. 25, 26.—Two Heads.

The war dance, of which I give an illustration, as showing tattooing on face and body, involved constant thrusting out of the tongue, and so much distortion of the features that the blue lines of the moko formed a quivering network. The time or cadence of the dance was marked by striking the palm of the left hand against the thigh.

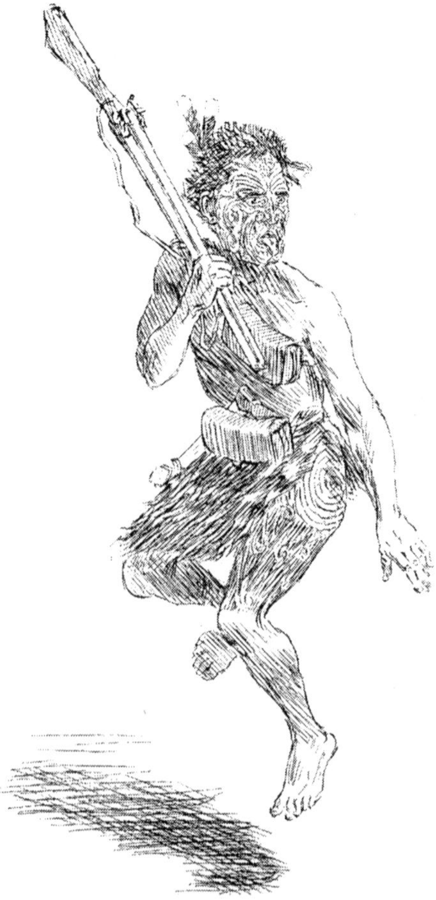

Fig. 27.—Moko in the War-dance.

CHAPTER III

MOKO WOMEN

Fashion and custom required among the Maoris that their women should also receive certain marks of moko; and these portraits fairly well indicate the extent to which this was practised. The lips and chin were the chief objects of attention to the artist in moko; and the idea seems to have been that the woman's lips should be not only *full* but *blue*—a combination which was regarded as the height of feminine beauty. It seems quite clear that a red lip was looked on as a reproach or disfigurement. The moko on the lips consisted of horizontal lines, as with the men.

Sydney Parkinson, already referred to as the artist with Captain Cook, says: "Of the women, their lips were in general stained of a blue colour, and several of them were scratched all over their faces as if it had been done with needles or pins."

And at another part of the coast he speaks of one woman who in particular was very curiously tattooed.

Rutherford (1816-26) says: "The women had a figure worked on the chin resembling an inverted crown; the inside of the lips was also tattooed, the figures on the lips appearing of a blue colour. They had also a mark on each side of the mouth as well as on the forehead and on each side of the nose."

Savage (1807) remarks on a small spiral figure on each side

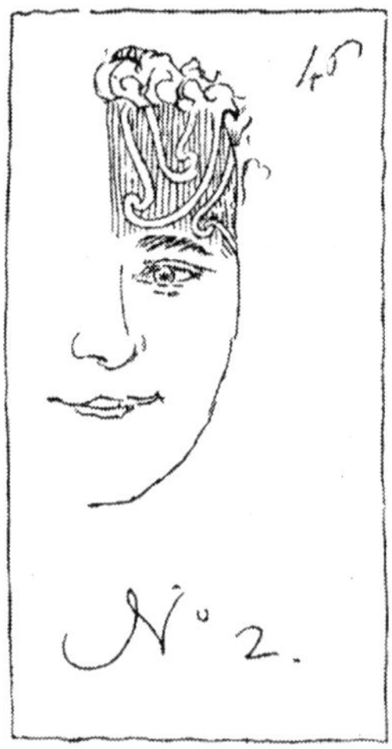

FIG. 28.—Curious tattooing on a girl's forehead.
(Captain Cook's "Voyages" from an original drawing in the British Museum, Additional Manuscripts Room.)

of the chin, a semicircular figure over each eyebrow, and two or three lines on each lip. Major Cruise, in a work published in 1824, states that the females were slightly tattooed upon the upper lip, centre of chin, and above the eyebrows, and that some had a few lines on their limbs. He mentions that a woman was seen at Shukehanga, up from the south, whose breast was marked with lines resembling the links of a chain; and that a female prisoner of Krokos was tattooed almost as much as a man. In confirmation of this, I may mention here that

Mr. Tregear speaks of some women in the South Island as being tattooed on the face like men. But this was very rare. Darwin (1835) tells us how certain native girls had remarked to missionaries' wives: "We really must have a few lines on our lips, else when we grow old our lips will shrivel up and we shall be ugly."

This last statement closely represents the object of moko

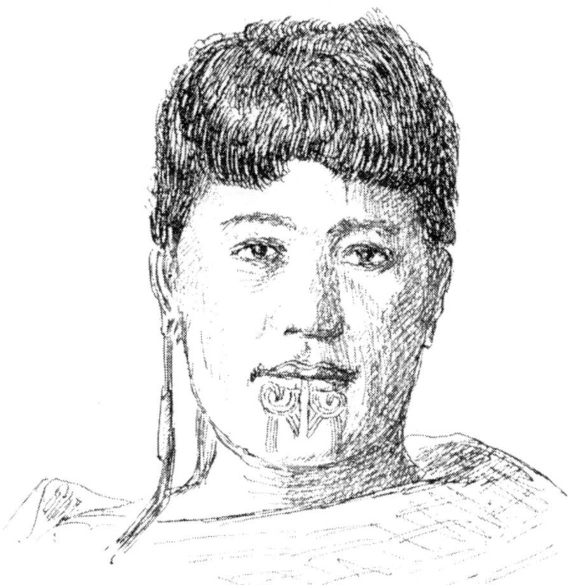

FIG. 29.—Usual tattooing on a Maori woman.

among the women; and a feeble parallel suggests itself in the painless patches with which European belles of the last century used to decorate their faces. I say "painless" for reasons which with regard to moko will be made apparent. Women of all

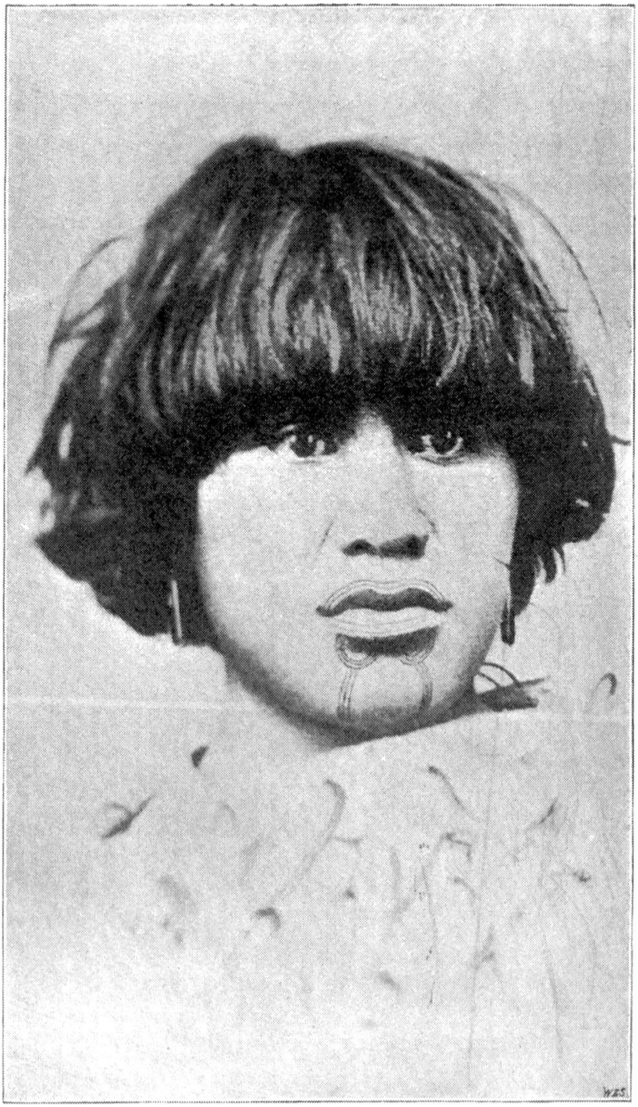

Fig. 30.—A Maori girl, showing two lines over upper lip, three on lower lip, and ornament on chin.

countries will submit to much inconvenience and some pain in order to satisfy the recognised standard of fashion for the time being; but it needs something like heroism to submit to the torture of moko, slight as the tattooing was in the case of most

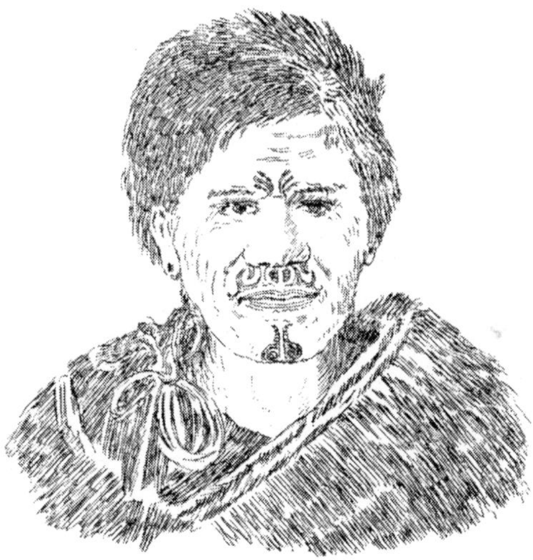

FIG. 31.—An old woman, well marked.
(From a drawing by the Author.)

native women in New Zealand. I remember seeing in 1865 a white woman, the wife of a native; her undecorated face showed that she had not undergone the painful process. A portrait of her husband, a sailor named Anaru, is sketched from life.[1] (Fig. 128.)

[1] In the memorable massacre of the people on board the ship *Boyd*, a little girl was saved. In later life she used to recount how during her captivity she received some blue marking on her lips. I mention this as an instance of a white woman tattooed.

Though custom permitted of only a small quantity of moko on the women's faces, there was no law against the elaboration of design on the rest of their persons, thighs and breast, with a few smaller marks on the different parts of the body as well. Mr. Savage says he believes children were not operated on by the artist until they were eight or ten years of age; but once begun, small moko strokes were frequently made all over their bodies. Sir Walter Buller, K.C.B., tells me that it was the

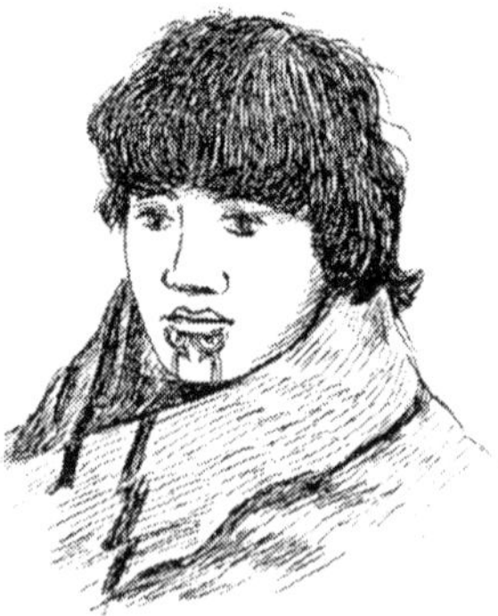

FIG. 32.—Tattooed young.

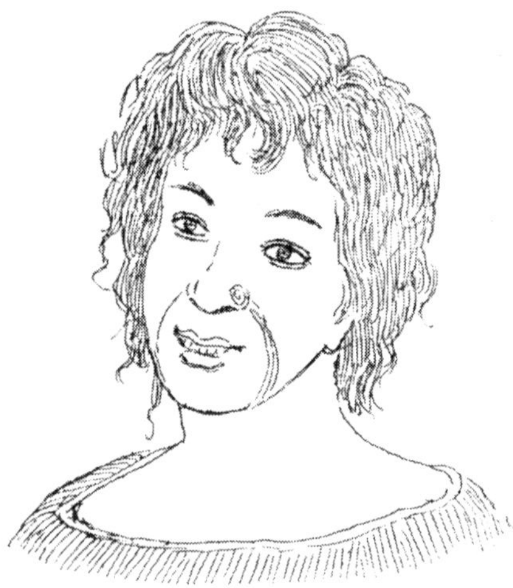

FIG. 33.—From Dumont D'Urville's "Voyages," c. 1826.

universal rule amongst the Maori never to commence moko until the subject was adult. Further growth would no doubt tend to distort the curved lines. As a matter of fact, Sir Walter says that in the whole course of his experience he has never seen a Maori boy or girl with a tattooed face. The famous

French traveller D'Urville says on this subject: "When I went with Tuai to visit the village of Taowera, the chief Tuao showed

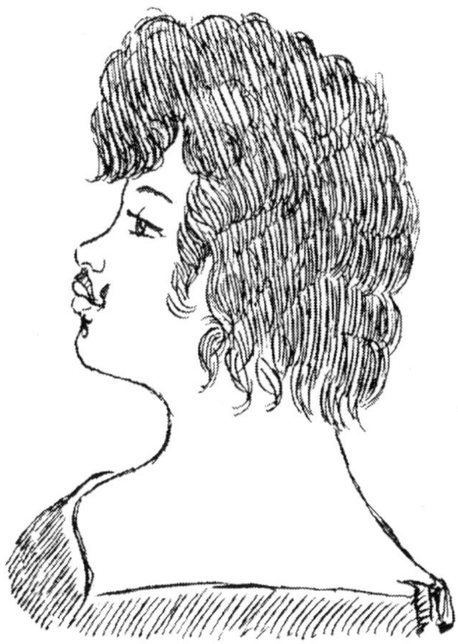

FIG. 34.—A girl's head from Dumont D'Urville's "Voyages."

FIG. 35.—The same, lip and chin.

me his wife while she was in the act of receiving the completion of her moko on the shoulders. Half of her back was already incised with deeply cut designs, similar to those which adorned the faces of Coro-Coro's relatives, and a female slave was engaged

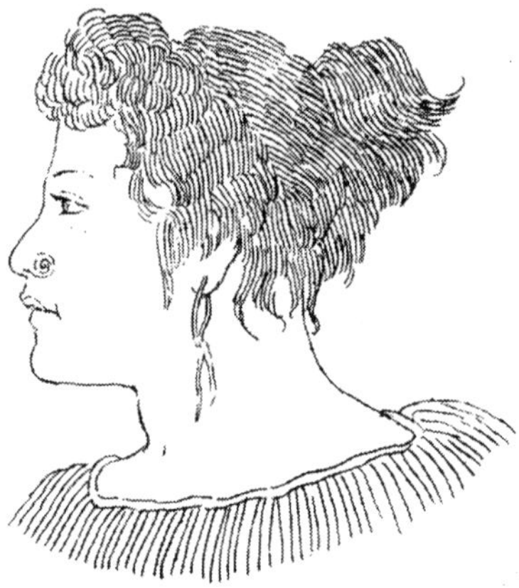

FIG. 36.—From Dumont D'Urville's "Voyages."

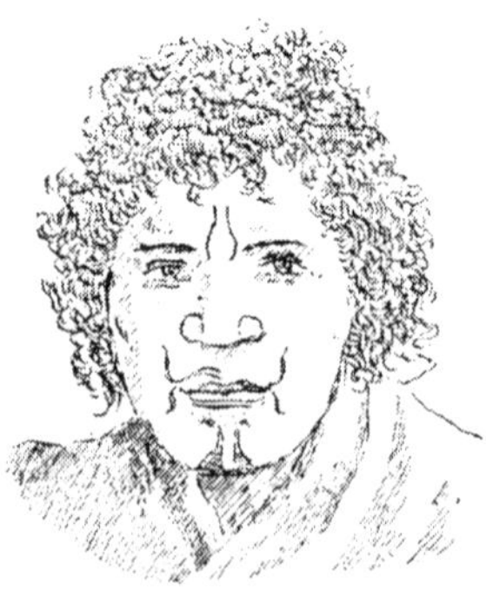

FIG. 37.—Curious tattooing on a Maori woman. (*From a drawing by the Author.*)

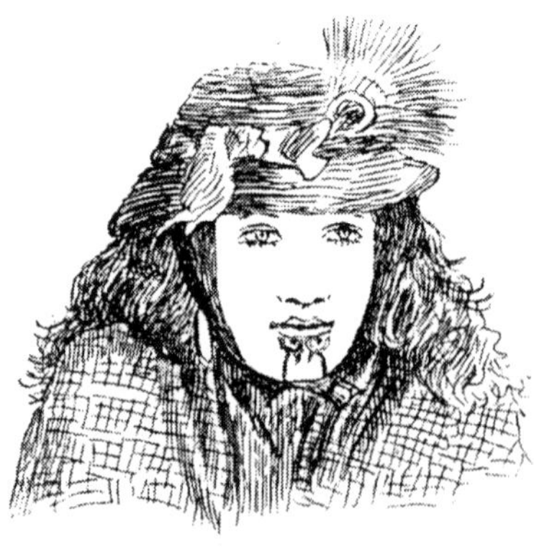

FIG. 38.—Half-caste girl. (*From a drawing by the Author.*)

in decorating the other side of the back with designs of like taste. The unfortunate woman was lying on her chest, and seemed to be suffering greatly, while the blood gushed forth abundantly from her shoulders. Still she did not even utter a sigh, and looked at me merrily with the greatest composure,

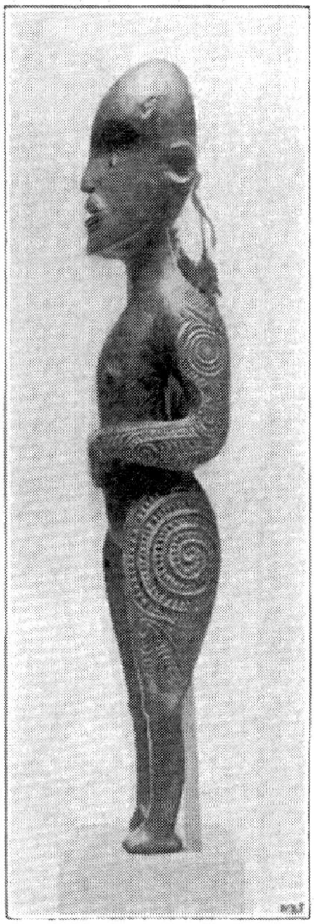

Fig. 39.—From a wooden effigy in the British Museum, showing thigh tattooing on a woman. The figure was presented by Sir A. W. Franks, K.C.B.

as did also the woman who was operating upon her. Tuao himself seemed to glory in the new honour his wife was receiving by these decorations."

And I find Mr. Tregear says that "in 'olden days' women were tattooed on the back part of the leg or calf." I shall have occasion to refer to the above account given by D'Urville in connection with the fact that in this instance the artist in moko was a woman.

In Mr. J. C. Bidwell's *Rambles in New Zealand* (1839)

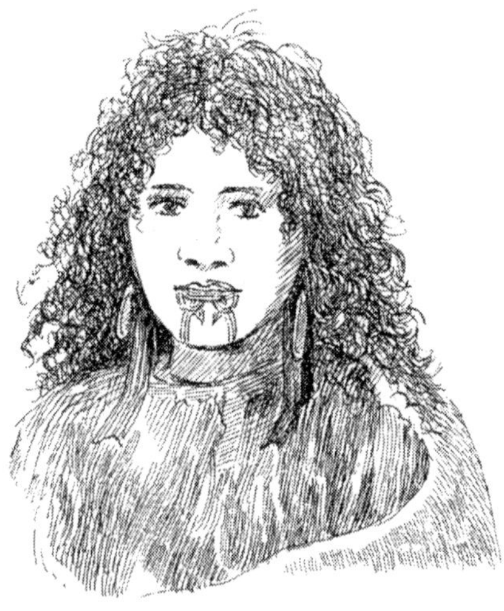

Fig. 40.—Right upper-lip unfinished.
(*From a drawing by the Author.*)

the following remarks on this singular aspect of the subject are to be found. He says: "While crossing one creek where we had to wade above half a mile, a native told me that one of the women was tattooed behind like the men. I asked her if it was the case, and she said yes, and if I would wait and let her get on a bit ahead she would show me, which she accordingly did, to my great edification. It is a very rare thing for women to be tattooed anywhere but about the lips and chin; and this was quite a curiosity. I used to think it very ornamental in the men, but what its use can be in a woman I cannot imagine, as they are always covered. The women are often quite covered with blue marks which might be called

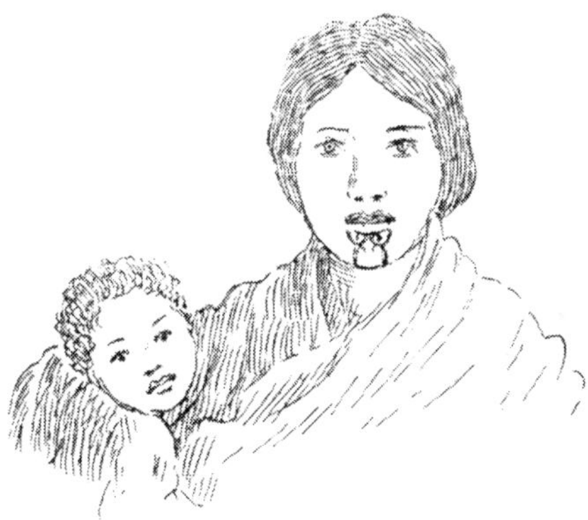

FIG. 41.—Half-caste and child.

tattooing in England; it is of the same kind as sailors are so fond of pricking into their arms; but it is a totally different thing to the elaborate engraving on a New Zealander's face or thigh; inasmuch as in one case the skin is cut and remains in the same pattern as the stains, and in the other the marks do not at all affect the smoothness of the skin. I have seen the arms and bodies of the New Zealand women so covered with these powerful blue marks that they looked as if they had on them a tight-fitting figured chintz dress."

And I will conclude my extracts from the travellers who

have noticed moko in New Zealand on women by a reference to Mr. Kerry Nicholls's (1884) mention of an albino woman in New Zealand, with light flaxen hair, pink eyes, and white complexion, with her lips marked in the ordinary manner, and also to a reference on the part of the same authority to a

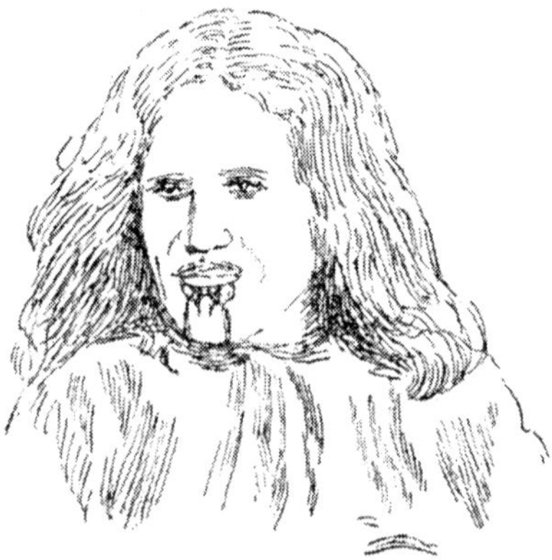

Fig. 42.—An Albino woman tattooed.

custom among the Maori women at Lake Taupo, which he says he had not noticed anywhere else. This consisted of tattooing the legs as well as the lips, in thin cross lines of a dark blue colour.

Another valuable piece of evidence is furnished by Mr. William Colenso. He says that the operator began on both sexes at about the age of puberty. In the female the tattooing was confined to the lips, chin, and space between the eyes and a little up the forehead, and on the back part of the leg from the heel to the calf. The last three mentioned tattooings are, he says, always indicative of rank. The women also were often irregularly marked on the hands, arms, breast, and face with small crosses, short lines, and dots. He says he saw very few women with faces tattooed like a man's; and these belonged to southern tribes, some of whom had a very different style of tattooing long ago, such as is shown in Plate XIII. in the quarto edition of Captain Cook's *Voyages*.

There was another form of marking among the Maori women which requires some mention. They are always the chief mourners at funerals. At every pause in their wailings and mournful cadence, the custom was in days gone by that they should gash their faces, necks, arms, and bodies with sharp shells until they streamed with blood; the *narahu* or moko-dye was sometimes applied to the wounds, and the stains commemorated the

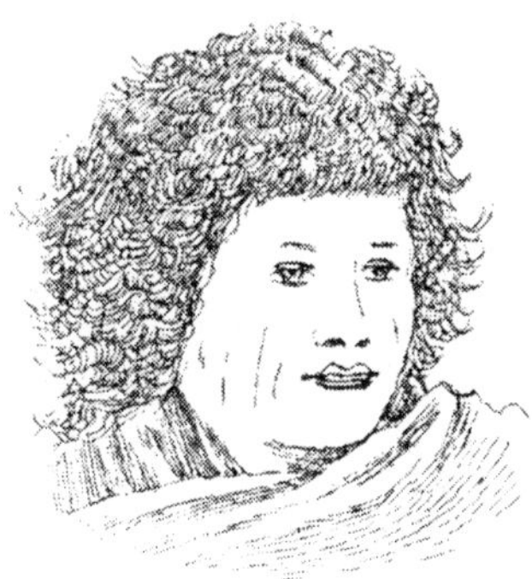

FIG. 43.—A sketch from Angas's book (1846) dyed lacerations at a mourning.

scenes at which the women assisted, the gashes making a sort of moko to perpetuate the signs of their grief. In Angas's book, *The New Zealanders Illustrated* (1846), there is a portrait of a woman whose skin has been thus gashed and dyed, and it is noticeable that she shows the more regular moko of women, the lower lip being carved and stained. Maning, to whom I have already referred, also gives a description of the laceration, in his *Old New Zealand.* He says: "One old woman had marked herself most conspicuously with a piece of volcanic glass, drawing the spouting blood. She had scored her forehead and cheeks before I came. . . . I noticed that the younger women,

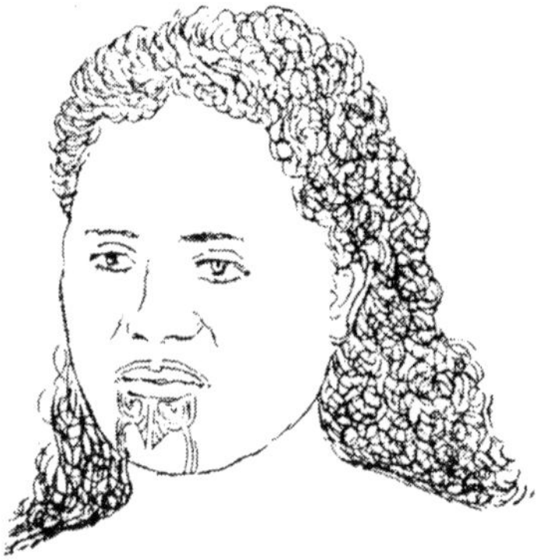

FIG. 44.—Portrait of a Maori girl.

although they screamed as loud, did not cut so deep as the old women, especially about the face."

There can be no doubt that in some of these wild scenes of mourning the cutting was done with considerable method and regularity, so as to make the scars ornamental rather than otherwise.

It should be added that an authority, A. W. Buckland, thinks the tattooed mark on the chin almost always denotes marriage. Of the present time (1896) it may be said that many Maori women still decorate themselves and that it suits them well.

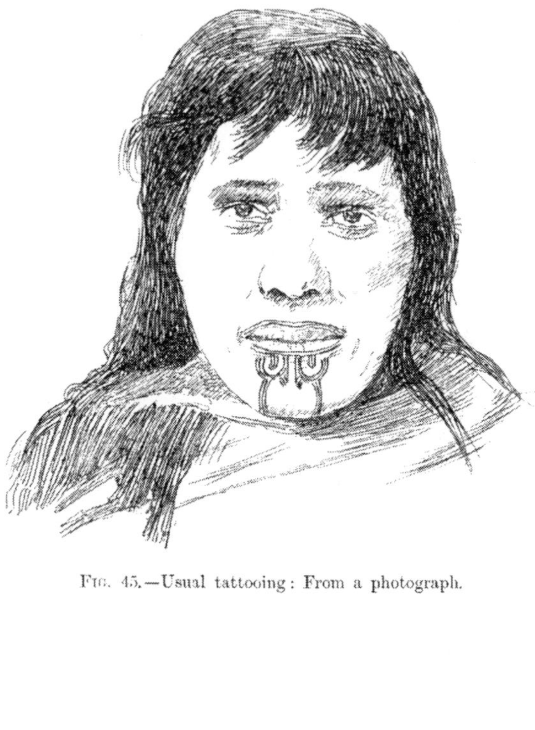

Fig. 45.—Usual tattooing: From a photograph.

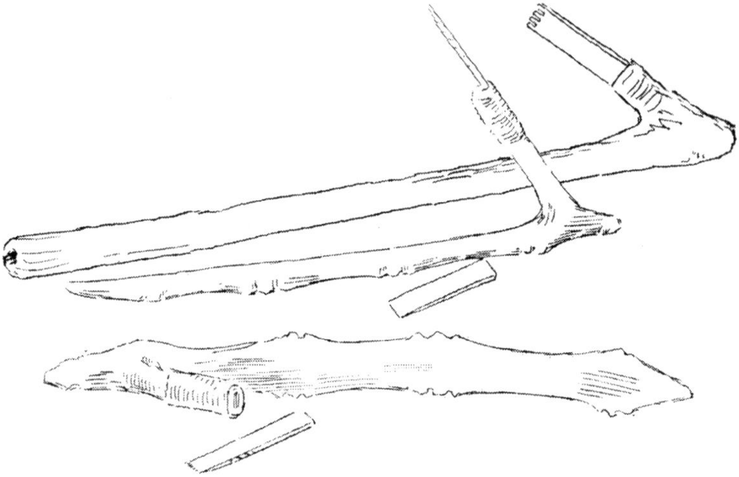

FIG. 46.—Uhi, or chisels in the British Museum (actual size). Presented by Sir George Grey, K.C.B., &c.

CHAPTER IV

MOKO PROCESSES

MOKO was a long and for the patient a painful operation. I have remarked on some of its attributes in the foregoing pages, and need not now repeat what has been said. In several points, however, additional and interesting information is forthcoming.

The instrument used for making the incisions in the flesh was called Uhi, and was very like a small narrow chisel. I give illustrations of some of these chisels preserved in the British Museum. Sometimes they had merely a sharp edge, others were furnished with comb-like teeth. The chisel was sometimes made from a sea-bird's wing-bone; some were made of sharks' teeth, stones, or hard wood, and were usually worked down to a fine edge or point. They were also of different sizes and shapes so that they could be applied to different parts of the flesh, and could be used for coarse or fine work as the case might be. The average breadth of the blade was about a quarter of an inch. The incision into the flesh was made by applying the edge to the skin, and driving it in by means of a smart

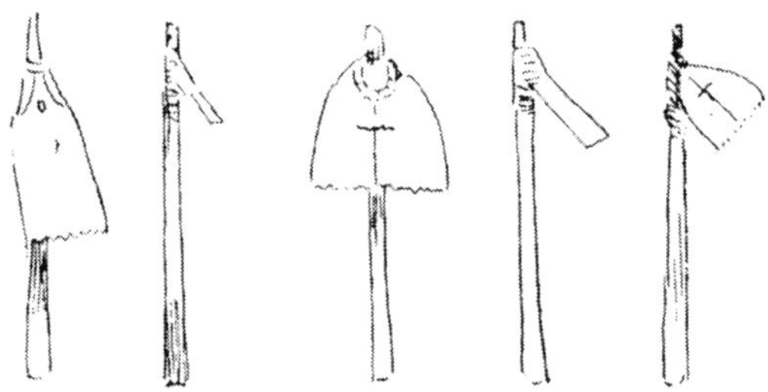

FIG. 47.—Tattooing instruments. (After Polack.)

tap applied to the handle with a small light mallet, thus causing a deep cut in the flesh. The mallet was called He Mahoe; sometimes it had a broad flattened surface at one end used to wipe away the blood that interfered with the artist's work. The artist sometimes held in his hand a piece of muka or flax dipped into the pigment, and this he applied to the incision as soon as it was made. The Uhi or chisel penetrated quite through the skin and sometimes, as the Rev. Mr. Taylor says, completely through the cheek as well; in which case when the patient took his pipe the smoke found its way out through the cuttings. The pain was of course excruciating, especially in the more tender parts, and caused dreadful swellings. New Zealand tattooing is rough to the touch and deep canals were made in the skin. Under the skin the black charcoal looks blue black, and time renders the pigment less dark. Since iron instruments were used the scars produced were however less rough.

When iron Uhi were introduced much finer work became possible; and thus Sheffield may be said to have something to do with the later development of the art.

Fitzroy mentions this finer work in 1835; Darwin, in the same year, and Wakefield, in the period 1839–44. As was natural, the natives most in contact with Europeans were the first to adopt the iron instrument. In the earliest days chisel work was the only method employed in tattooing; but later on the system of pricking was introduced and allowed the artist far more scope for his elaboration of detail. The general practice of operators in moko undoubtedly was however to dip the Uhi or chisel into the colouring matter before incising the skin, so that the process of cutting and colouring went on at the ame time; the chisel was then withdrawn, wiped clean, and dipped again in the pigment for another insertion. Polack says: "The process was one of intense pain, the recumbent figure of the victim wincing and writhing at every stroke of the operator and quivering under the torments inflicted." The sufferer looked very hideous after the operation, and instances were even known of permanent distortion of the features.

An excellent description of the process (at the date 1839–44) is furnished by Mr. Wakefield: "I saw Iwikau or 'the Skeleton,' the head fighting chief of the tribe under Heu-heu, being chipped on the cheek-bone. The instruments used were not of bone as they used formerly to be, but a graduated set of iron tools fitted with handles like adzes supplied their place. The man spoke to me with perfect nonchalance for a quarter of an hour, although the operator continued to strike

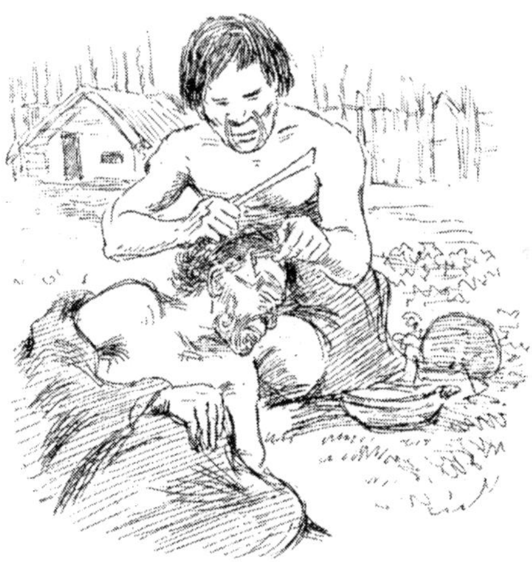

Fig. 48.—Tattooing a head.

the little adzes into his flesh with a light wooden hammer the whole time, and his face was covered with blood. The worst part of the pain seems to be endured a day or two after the operation, when every part of the wound gathers and the face is swollen considerably. The staining liquid is made of charcoal. I rarely saw a case in which the scars were not completely well in a week."

Another good account is as follows: "The instrument used to make the punctures is formed out of a piece of whalebone, according to the design intended to be cut, and is bound to a piece of wood in the shape of a carpenter's square. This the tohunga holds in his left hand between his forefinger and thumb. In his right hand between his third and fourth finger is held a piece of fern-stalk, about eight inches long, the outer end of which is bound with a little flax. Between the thumb and forefinger of the same hand is held the black; when the tohunga has made an incision with the Uhi by striking it with the piece of fern-stalk held in his right hand, he again draws the Uhi between the finger and thumb which holds the black, and in so doing it carries with it a portion for the next incision."

From this I will pass to Rutherford's earlier account, which is of deep interest, though I doubt if the whole operation could have been undergone at one "sitting" as he seems to suggest. Rutherford and five of the crew of the *Agnes* were captured by the Maoris in 1816; and he remained a prisoner close on ten years.

"The whole of the natives having then seated themselves on the ground in a ring, we were brought into the middle and, being stripped of our clothes and laid on our backs, we were each of us held down by five or six men, while two others commenced the operation of tattooing us. Having taken a bit of charcoal and rubbed it upon a stone with a little water until they had produced a thickish liquid, they then dipped into it an instrument made of bone, having a sharp edge like a chisel and shaped in the fashion of a garden hoe, and immediately applied it to the skin, striking it twice or thrice with a small piece of wood. This made it cut into the flesh as a knife would have done, and caused a great deal of blood to flow which they kept wiping off with the side of the hand, in order to see if the impression was sufficiently clear. When it was not they applied the bone a second time to the same place. They employed, however, various instruments in the course of the operation; one which they sometimes used being made of a shark's tooth, and another having teeth like a saw. They had them also of different sizes to suit different parts of the work. While I was undergoing the operation, although the pain was most acute, I never either moved or uttered a sound, but my comrades moaned dreadfully. . . . . Although the operators were very quick and dexterous, I was four hours under their hands, and during the operation Aimy's (a chief) eldest daughter several times wiped the blood from my face with some dressed flax. After it was over she led me to the river that I might wash myself (for it had made me completely blind). . . . and then conducted me to a great fire. They now returned us all our clothes with the exception of our shirts, which the women kept for themselves, wearing them, as we observed, with the fronts behind. In three days the swelling which had been produced by the operation had greatly subsided and I began to recover my sight; but it was six weeks before I was completely well. I had no medical assistance of any kind during my illness."

The description Rutherford gives agrees with that of other observers; though it is generally concluded that in no case is the operation undergone at once, as appears to have been his experience.

Captain Cruise asserts that the tattooing in New Zealand is occasionally renewed as the lines become fainter by time; and that one of the chiefs who returned home was re-tattooed soon

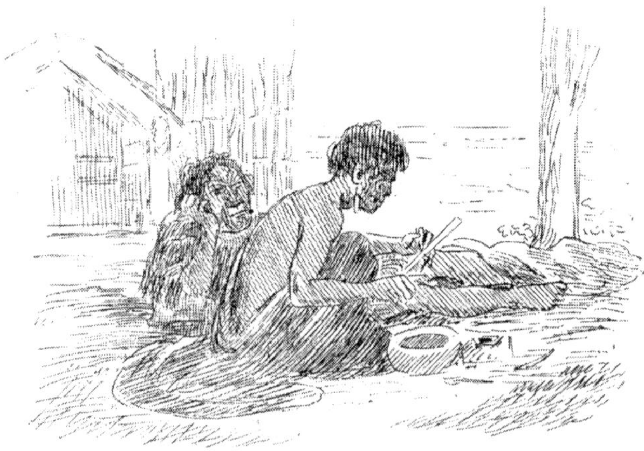

FIG. 49.—Tattooing a thigh. (After Earle.)

after his arrival. Both this authority and Mr. Marsden expressly state that according to their information it always required several months and sometimes years to complete the tattoo of a chief; and that this was so because of the necessity of allowing one part of the face or body to heal before operating on another. Perhaps, too, the prolongation of the process may have been necessary where the amoco is of more intricate pattern, or the surface operated on was larger than that which Rutherford describes; or in his particular case it may have been determined to test his powers of endurance further than would have been necessary in the case of a native. The portrait of Rutherford well represents the tattooing on his body. I will complete the story of Rutherford's experiences later on; but will say here that he has omitted to mention the tracing out of the figure on the flesh prior to the cutting of the skin. This appears to have been invariable in New Zealand and elsewhere. According to Mr. Savage a piece of burnt stick or red earth was used for the purpose.

To tattoo a person fully was, in fact, a matter of time; and if too much was attempted at once it positively endangered life. The Rev. Mr. Taylor tells us of a poor porangi, or lunatic, who during a war was tattooed most unmercifully by some young scoundrels, and his wounds became so inflamed as to occasion death. When once the operation has been performed, it is not possible to erase the moko; not sickness nor death itself has the power of destroying. When a head was preserved every line retained its distinctness; and appeared almost more distinct than when subject to alteration from the muscular motions of the living man.

Letourneau (1881) gives two modes of tattooing. The first, he says, is that done with a sharp stone or a shark's tooth; the second, with a small instrument with sharp teeth. Tattooing by means of cutting is, he says, still the method most employed by the New Zealanders; but the system of pricking allows of more adornment and of an enlargement of the primitive custom. Much importance is, he says, attached to this form of ornamentation which is shown chiefly on the face. It is made by winding arabesques showing off the different features of the face, and is often done with considerable skill.

And now with regard to the pigment or dye with which the

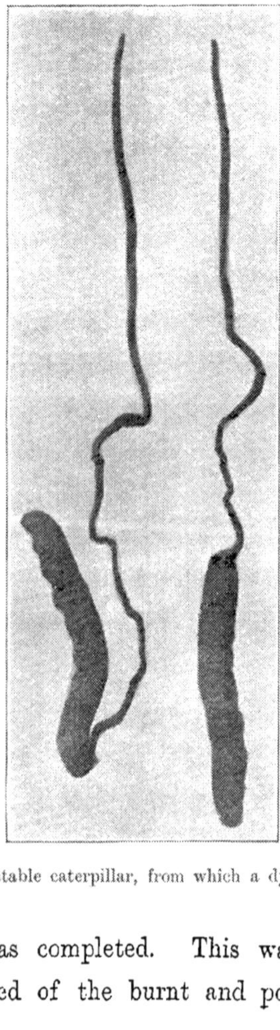

FIG. 50.—Vegetable caterpillar, from which a dye is obtained.

process of moko was completed. This was called Narahu or Kapara, and consisted of the burnt and powdered resin of the

Kauri pine, Kahikatea, or of Koromico, a veronica. This was said to give the finest tint to the moko, always a blue-black. Aweto Hotete, or vegetable caterpillar, burnt, was also sometimes employed. This plant is a native of New Zealand, and amongst the most remarkable productions on the border line between the vegetable and animal kingdoms. The caterpillar burrowing in the vegetable soil gets a spore of a fungus between the folds of its neck; and, unable to free itself, the insect's body nourishes the fungus which vegetates and occasions the death of the caterpillar by exactly filling the interior of the body with its roots, always preserving its perfect form. The stem grows up like a little bulrush, six to ten inches in height; after being dried, it is burnt into a coal giving an excellent black pigment. Charcoal, too, and even gunpowder have been employed to yield the necessary colour. "At Taupo," says the Rev. Mr. Taylor, "I went to see the place where this pigment was manufactured; a narrow pit was sunk at a little distance from a precipice, and from the face of the cliff a passage was cut to the bottom of it, over the mouth of which pieces of wood containing the resin were burnt; the residuum falling within it was taken away."

Sometimes, however, the preparation was rubbed on a stone, and a little water was added to form a thin paste.

Another account gives the following information: "The soot with which they are marked is obtained by making a hole, somewhat like a lime-kiln, in which kauri (to burn black) gum is burnt, or a wood called kapara; on the top of the kiln is placed a Maori basket, made of korari besmeared with fat, to which the soot adheres. The black thus obtained is sacred, and is kept for generations, father and son being tattooed from the black made at one burning. The soot is mixed with oil or dog's fat."

Gunpowder has often been substituted, leaving a blue mark which time can never wholly efface.

As if the physical torture of moko were not sufficient to set the seal of true martyrdom on a Maori, he was subjected during the operation to a species of boycott or Tapu. He was forbidden all communication with people not in the same condition as himself; and in eating was not allowed to use his hands, and was dependent on his attendants for his food. According to the old superstition the man who presumed to raise a finger to his mouth before his moko was finished for the time would certainly find his stomach invaded by the Atua or fiend, who would devour him alive. Earle notices this. He says: "All those chiefs who were under the operating hands of Aranghie the tattooer were under the law. In fact, as we strolled through the village at the time of their evening repast, it appeared as though some dreadful disease had suddenly struck the greater part of the inhabitants and deprived them of the use of their limbs, most of them being either fed by their slaves, or lying flat on the ground and with their mouths eating out of their platters or baskets."

And Mr. E. Tregear says that a person being tattooed was prohibited from eating fish, unless the fish which is sacred to Tangaroa, the Sea-God, is held up to see the tattooing. No gourd or calabash might be eaten if children had playfully made tattooing marks thereon. Mr. Taylor too has some interesting remarks on this phase of the subject.

"During the time of the tapu," says the Rev. Mr. Taylor, "he could not be touched by any one, nor even put his own hand to his head; but he was either fed by another who was appointed for the purpose, or took up his food with his mouth from a small

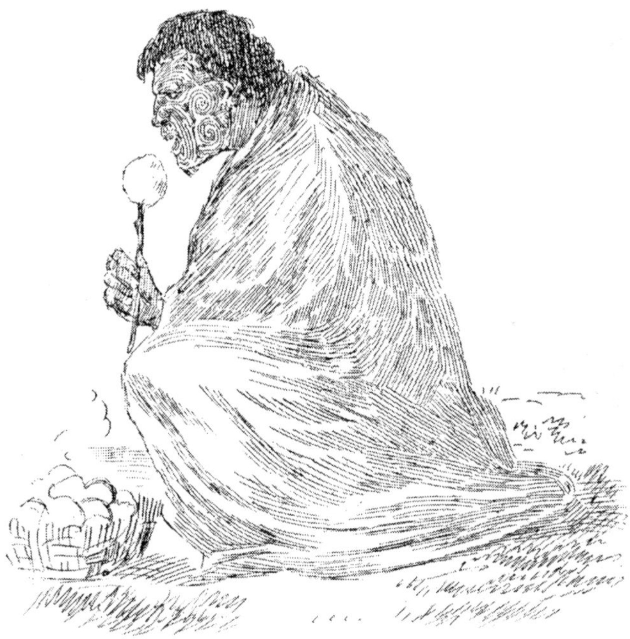

Fig. 51.—Tapued chief eating with a fern-stalk. (After Taylor.)

stage with his hands behind him, or by a fern-stalk, and thus conveyed it to his mouth. In drinking water, the water was poured in a very expert manner from a calabash into his mouth, or on his hands when he needed it for washing; so that he should not touch the vessel which otherwise could not have been used again for ordinary purposes."

Rutherford recounts the fate of one of his tattooed companions left with him. He says: "My comrade and I were left at home with nobody but a few slaves and the chief's mother, an old woman who was sick and attended by a physician. A physician in this country remains with his patients constantly both day and night, never leaving them till they either recover or die. . . . During the absence of the family at the feast, my comrade

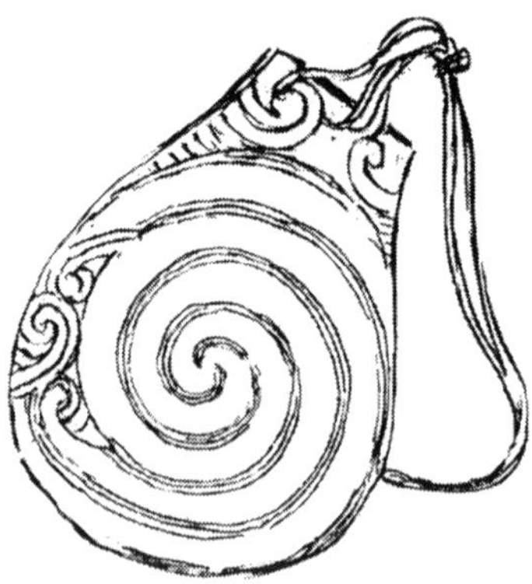

FIG. 52.—A tattooed gourd.
(*British Museum.*)

chanced to lend his knife to a slave for him to cut some rushes with in order to repair a house; and when this was done he received it back again. Soon after he and I killed a pig, from which we cut a portion into small pieces and put them into our own pot along with some potatoes which we had also peeled with our knives. When the potatoes were cooked the old woman who was sick desired us to give her some, which we did in the presence of the doctor, and she ate them. Next morning she died, when the chief and the rest of the family immediately returned home

. . . . On the third day after the death they all, to the number of some hundreds, proceeded to cut themselves. The following morning the men armed and alone formed a circle round the dead body, and the doctor appeared walking backwards and forwards in the ring. By this time my companions and I had learned a good deal of the language; and as we stood listening to what was said we heard the doctor relate the particulars of the old woman's illness and death: after which the chiefs began to inquire very closely into what she had eaten for the three days. At last, the doctor having retired from the ring, an old chief stepped forward with three or four white feathers stuck in his hair, and having walked several times up and down in the ring addressed the meeting and said that in his opinion the old woman's death had been occasioned by her having eaten potatoes that had been peeled with a white man's knife after it had been used for cutting rushes to repair a house; on which account he though that the white man to whom the knife belonged should be killed, which would be a great honour conferred upon the memory of the dead woman. To this proposal many of the other chiefs expressed their assent, and it seemed about to be adopted by the court. Meanwhile my companion stood trembling and unable to speak from fear. I then went forward myself into the ring and told them that if the white man had done wrong in lending his knife to the slave he had done so ignorantly, not knowing the customs of the country. I ventured to address myself to Aimy, beseeching him to spare my comrade's life; but he continued to keep his seat on the ground, mourning for the loss of his mother, without answering me or seeming to take any notice of what I said; and while I was yet speaking to him the chief with the white feathers went and struck my comrade on the head with a *mery* and killed him. Aimy however would not allow him to be eaten. The slaves therefore having dug a grave for him he was interred after my directions."

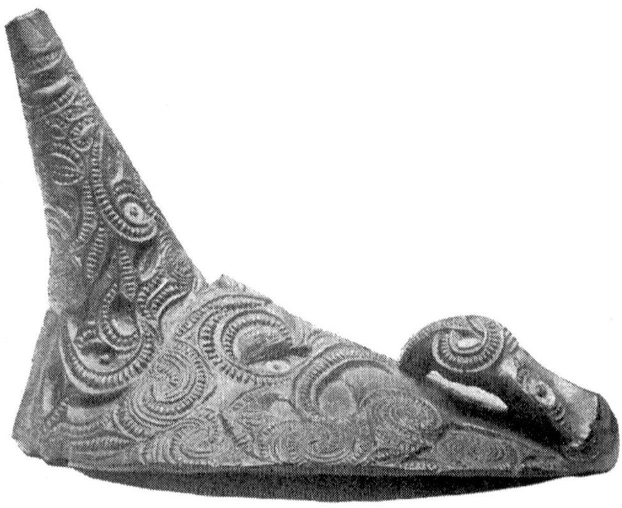

FIG. 53.—Funnel for feeding a chief during time of tattooing.
(*In Author's collection.*)

The religious character of these observances is brought into prominence by Polack who, speaking of "old times," says: "The priest and all the people are tapu (on account of the blood) during the operation; but the ceremony of making native ovens with hot stones is gone through—priest's oven, God's oven, and oven for the tattooed man. The priest handles one of the hot stones of the God's oven, thus transferring the tapu to their food which is hung up on a tree. After eating, all are *noa* (common, not tapu)."

And Rutherford, speaking of himself and five comrades, says: "We were not only tattooed, but what they called tabooed; the meaning is, 'made sacred' or forbidden to touch any provisions of any kinds with our hands. This state of things lasted three days, during which time we were fed by the daughters of the chiefs with the same victuals and out of the same baskets as the chiefs themselves and the persons who had tattooed us."

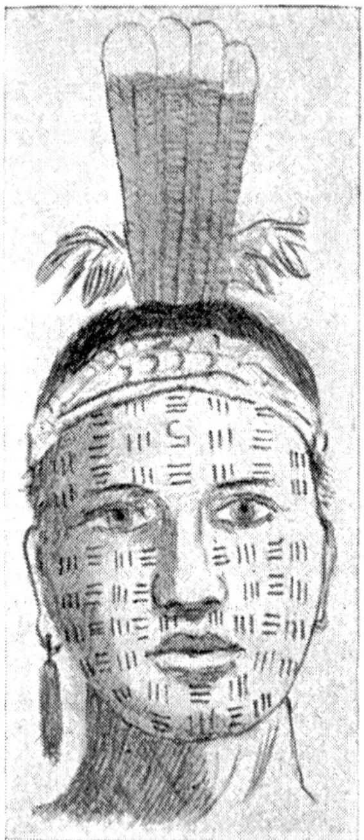

FIG. 54.—Ancient Moko pattern called Moko Kuri in Mr. J. White's book.

CHAPTER V

PATTERNS

ONE of the earliest patterns I can trace is that mentioned in Mr. J. White's book on the ancient history of the Maori. One illustration represented in the frontispiece gives the ancient tattoo pattern called "Moko Kuri." This consists of sets of three short lines successively, each set at right angles to its neighbour thus ||| ═ with a variant in the form of ƨ in the middle of the forehead. This is a great contrast to the ultimate development of the art, when the winding arabesques of the device in the forms they took were not merely designed to ornament a surface of flesh, but in parts followed the conformation of the individual countenance. Fitzroy comments on "the

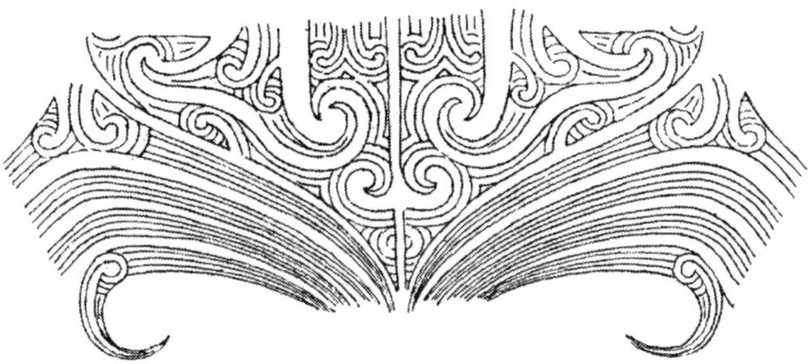

FIG. 55.—A forehead, author's collection.

taste and even elegance" of "such disfiguring devices." With regard to the effect of the art on those who grew accustomed

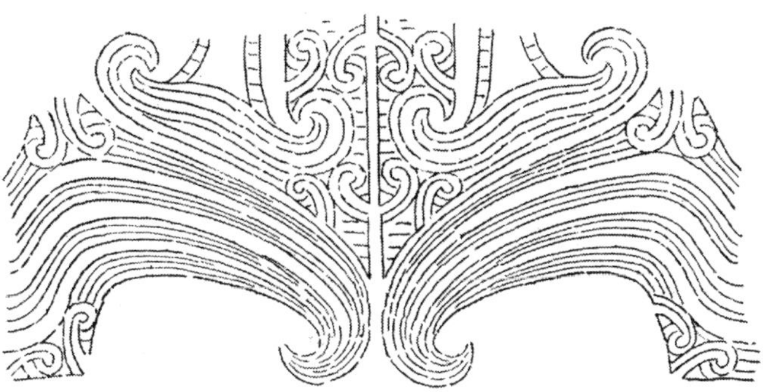

FIG. 56.—A forehead.

to it, I may mention that Darwin comments on the feeling it gave rise to. The Maori regarded the unmokoed face as common or plebeian; and writing in 1835 he says: "So soon does any train of ideas become habitual that the missionaries told me even in their eyes a plain face looked mean and not like a New Zealand gentleman."

And Earle, too, says: "The art was brought to such perfection that whenever we saw a New Zealander whose skin was thus

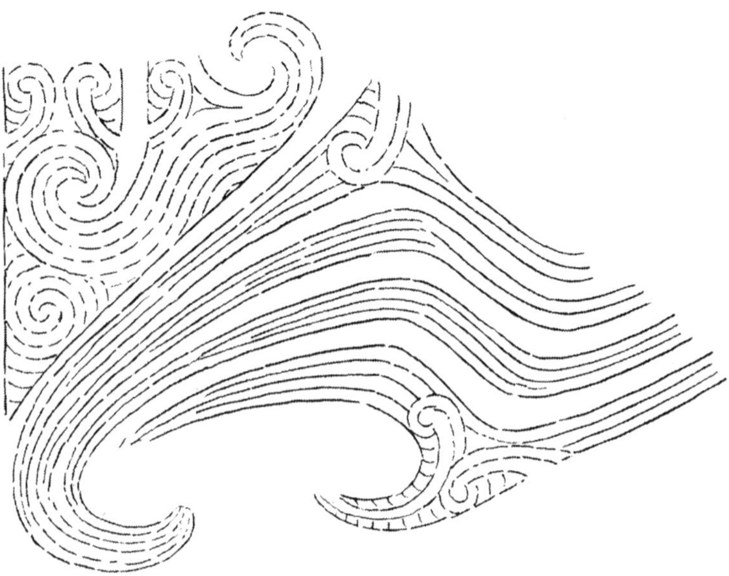

Fig. 57.—Left half of a forehead.
(*Author's collection.*)

ornamented we have admired him." Dieffenbach said the Waikato tribe was celebrated for their skill in the perfect execution of the designs.

I will first give the Rev. Mr. Taylor's list of nineteen Maori names for the different portions of the work of tattooing. It

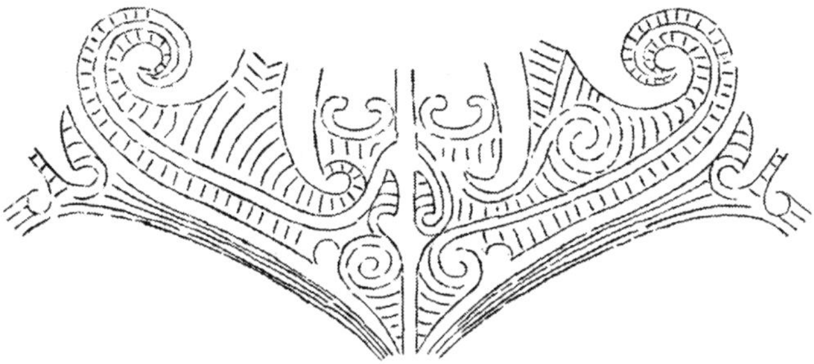

Fig. 58.—A forehead, showing signs of *post-mortem* work, over living work. (*Author's collection.*)

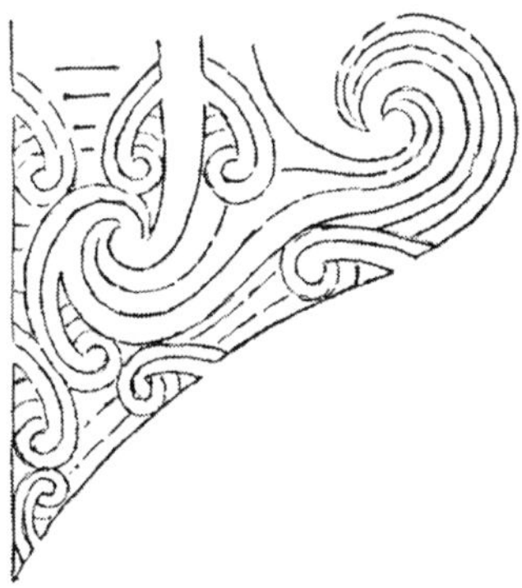

Fig. 59.—Left half of forehead. (*British Museum.*)

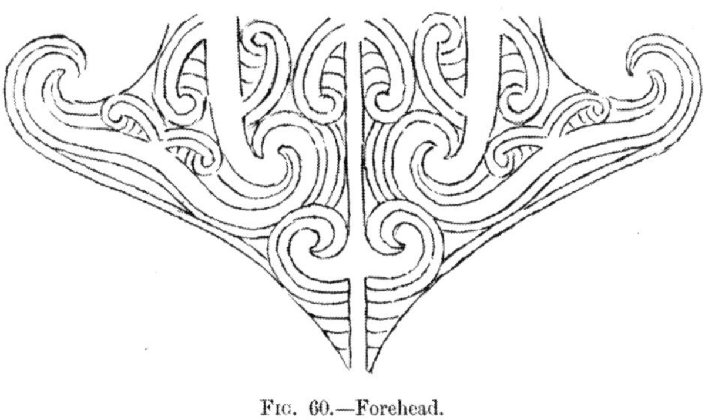

Fig. 60.—Forehead. (*From a wooden effigy in British Museum.*)

was subject to certain rules or systematic working; beginning at one part of the face or flesh and proceeding very gradually to

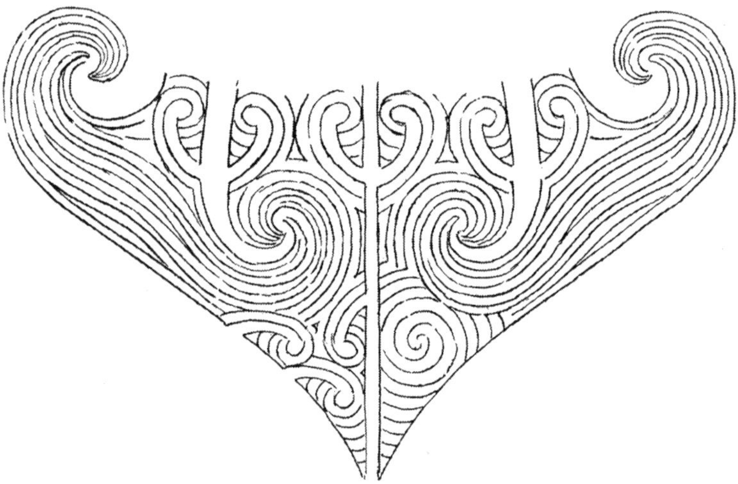

FIG. 61.—Variety in scroll work on forehead; a good specimen.
(*In Author's collection.*)

another, each set of markings having its distinctive name. Thus a beginning was made, according to that author, with—

TE KAWE, six lines on each side of chin.

TE PUHAWAE, lines on the chin.

NGA REPE HUPE, six lines below nostrils.

NGA KOKIRI, curved line on cheek-bone.

NGA KOROAHA, lines between cheek-bone and ear.

NGA WAKARAKAU, lines below cheek-bone and ear.

NGA PONGIANGIA, lines on each side of lower part of the nose.

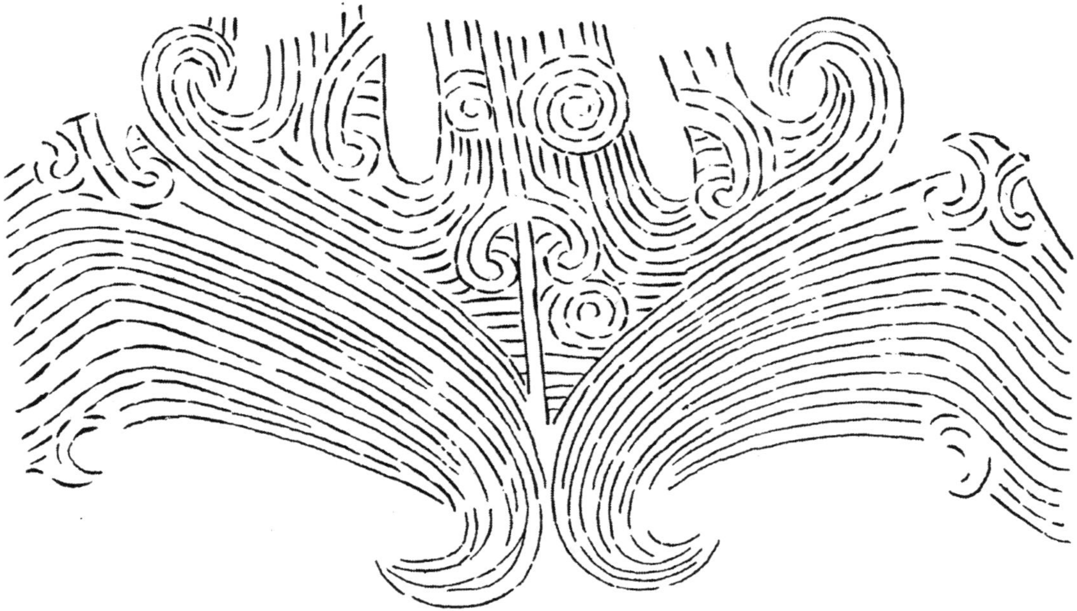

FIG. 62.—Specimen of coarse moko on forehead; lop-sided or irregular work.
(*Author's collection.*)

NGA PAE TAREWA, lines on the cheek-bone.

NGA REREPI and NGA NGATAREWA, lines on bridge of nose.

NGA TIWANA, four lines on forehead.

NGA REWHA, three lines below eyebrows.

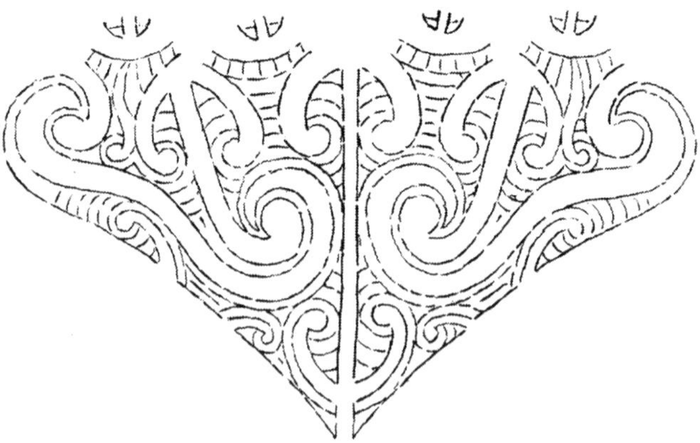

FIG. 63.—Forehead.
(Royal Coll. of Surgeons.)

NGA TITI, lines on centre of forehead.

TE TONOKAI, the general name for the lines on the forehead. (This name is derived from the movement made when a person assents to the inquiry if he wants food cooked for him by raising the eyebrows.)

HE NGUTU PU RUA, both lips tattooed.

TE RAPE, the higher part of the thighs.

TE PAKI PAKI, on the seat.

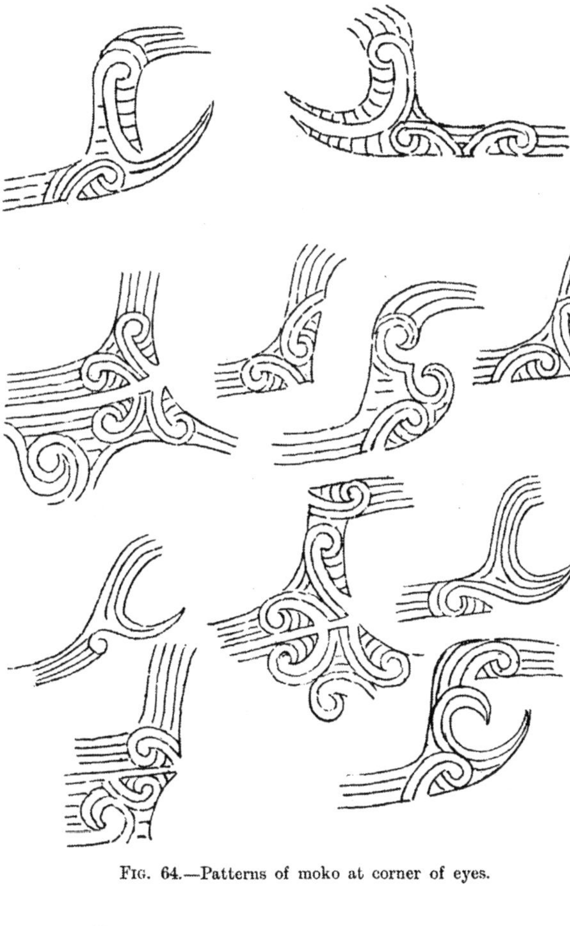

Fig. 64.—Patterns of moko at corner of eyes.

Te Paki Turi, lower thigh.

Nga Tata, the adjoining parts.

And the following are, according to the same authority, female tattoos:

Taki Taki, lines from the breast.

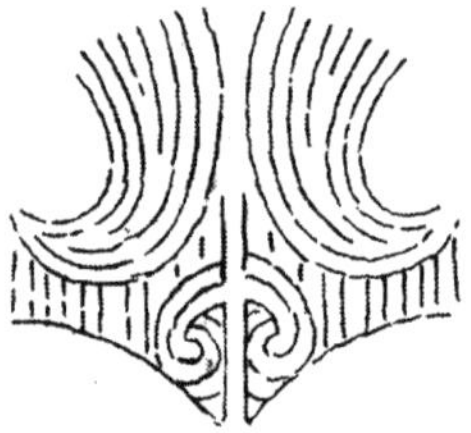

Fig. 65.—Marking over bridge of nose.

(*Royal Coll. of Surgeons.*)

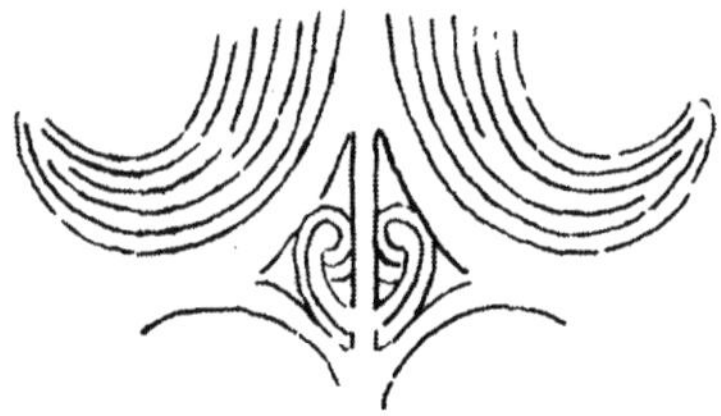

Fig. 66.—Over the nose.

(*Royal Coll. of Surgeons.*)

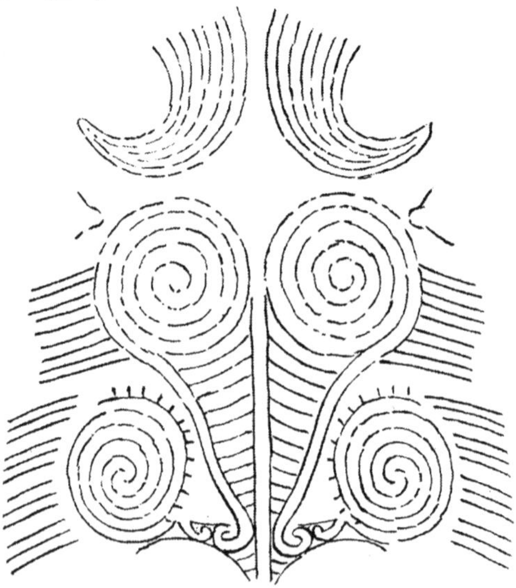

Fig. 67.—Nose tattooing.

(*Author's collection.*)

Hope Hope, lines on the thighs.

Waka Te He, lines on the chin.

I print this list of terms as being an essential part of a subject the memory of which is rapidly dying out. Every line had its name, which corresponded even among distant tribes, though the figures tattooed were not consistently made up of the same number of lines.

It will be readily seen that certain features are common to all

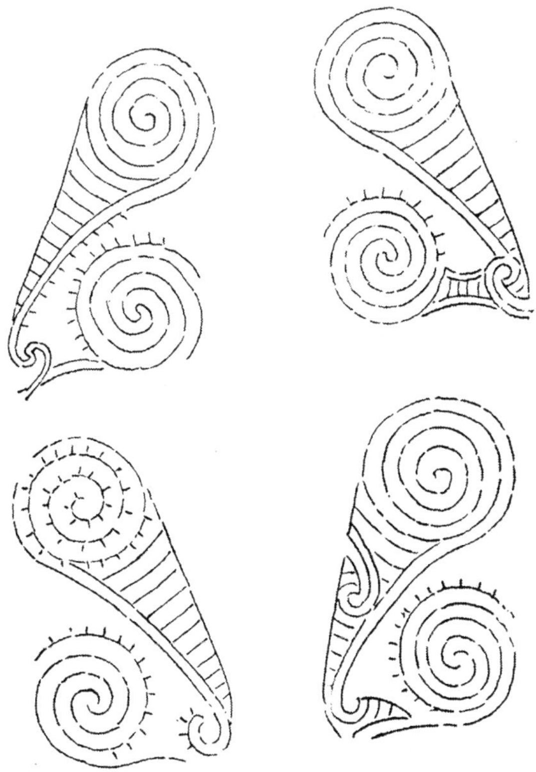

FIG. 68.—Various patterns on noses.

the moko patterns and designs, so that one fully tattooed man looked at a distance ornamented like another. On the forehead

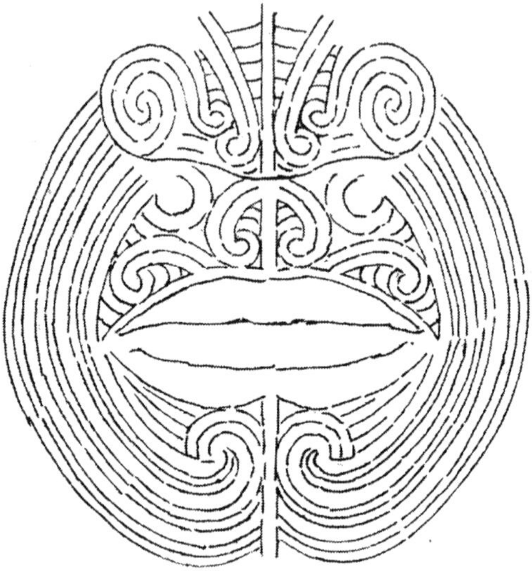

FIG. 69.—Upper lip and chin.

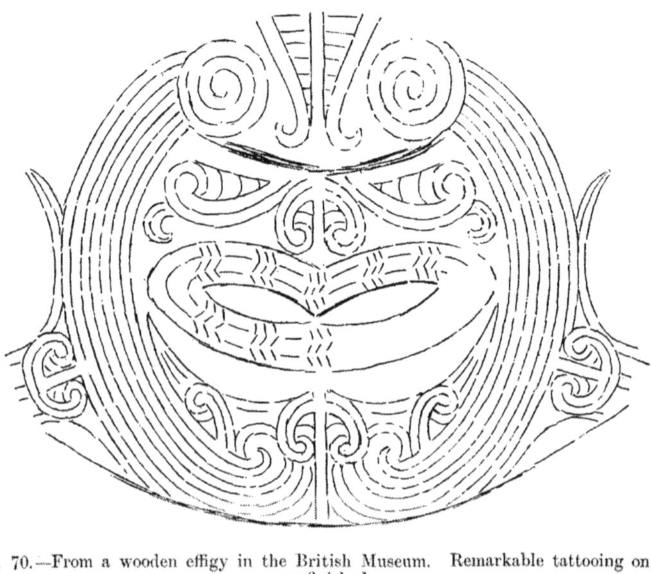

FIG. 70.—From a wooden effigy in the British Museum. Remarkable tattooing on lips, unfinished.

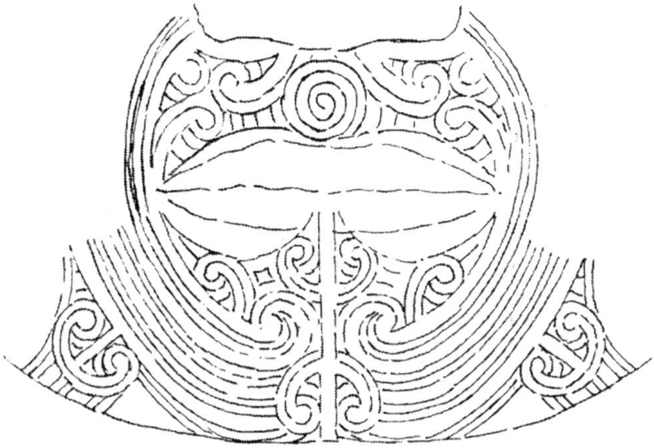

Fig. 71.—Upper lip and chin.

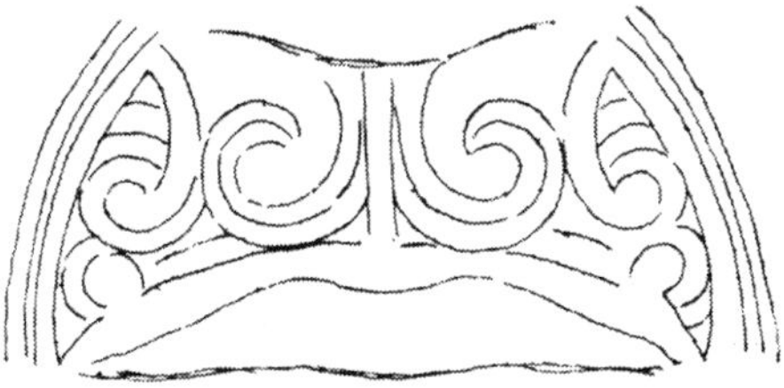

Fig. 72.—Over upper lip.

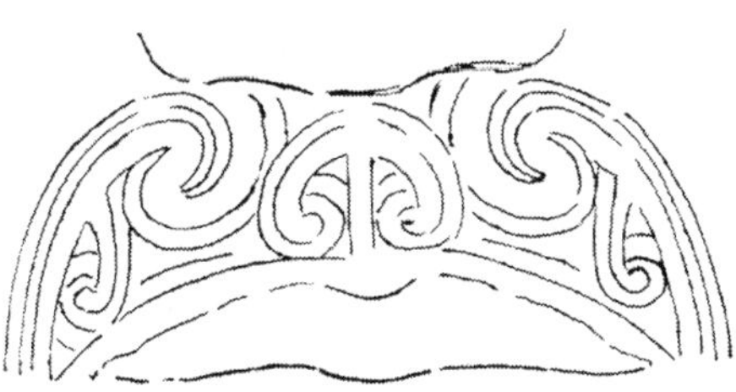

Fig. 73.—Over upper lip.

are eight bars radiating, and a V-shaped centre receives some curls. The nose also has its central ornament and spirals at bridge

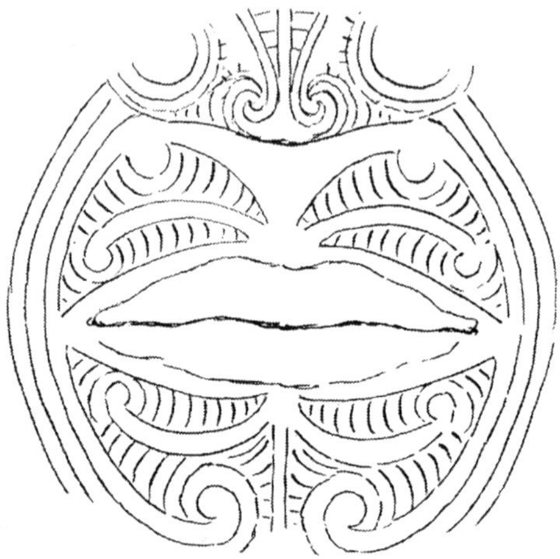

FIG. 74.—Upper lip and chin.
(*Author's collection.*)

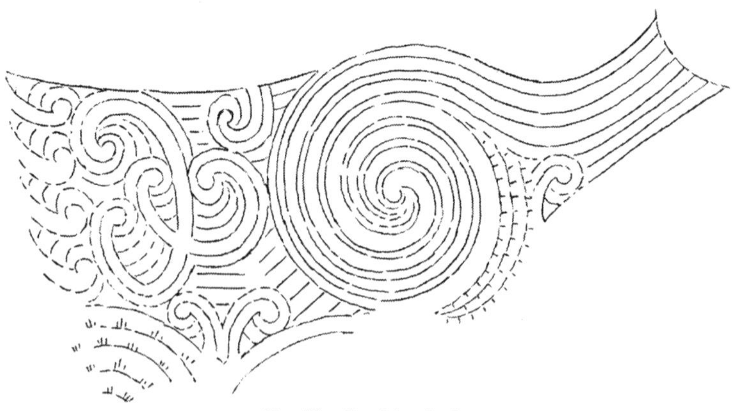

FIG. 75.—On right cheek.
(*Author's collection.*)

and nostrils, with an added ornament above, and a little variation at the tip of the nose. From the nose to the chin on either side are four or sometimes three sets of lines passing the corner of the mouth like a parenthesis. The upper lip has, least frequently, its suitable and varied patterns, the lips themselves having horizontal scoring. The cheek or jaw is decorated with

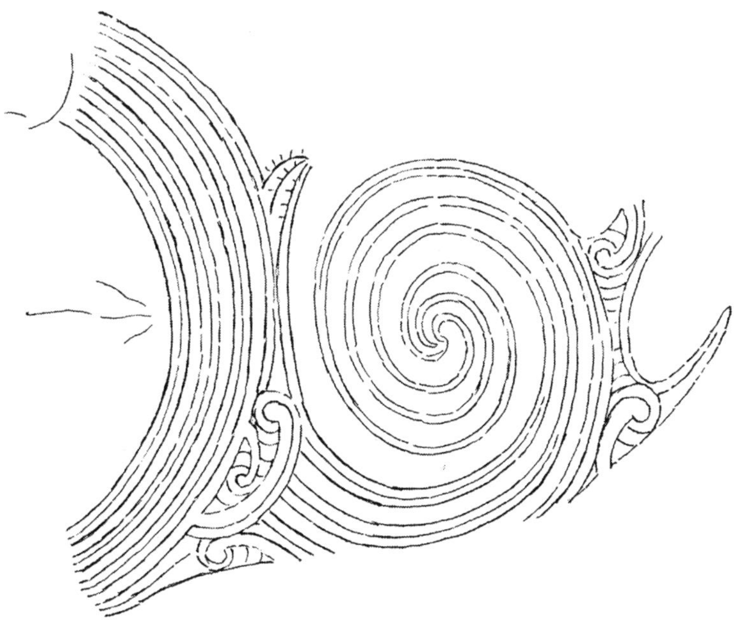

FIG. 76.—Lines from nostrils to chin, from the outer line commences the lower spiral on jaw. (*Author's collection.*)

spirals; and sometimes in the older specimens bands of tattooing go across one or both sides of the face.

On the chin and near the ears the fancy of the artist-operator has fuller play, and gives more artistic tracery. I have taken more pains to copy this latter as in the full face or in three-quarter face portraits it cannot be seen. The patterns extend from the throat to the roots of the hair; before the operation every hair that

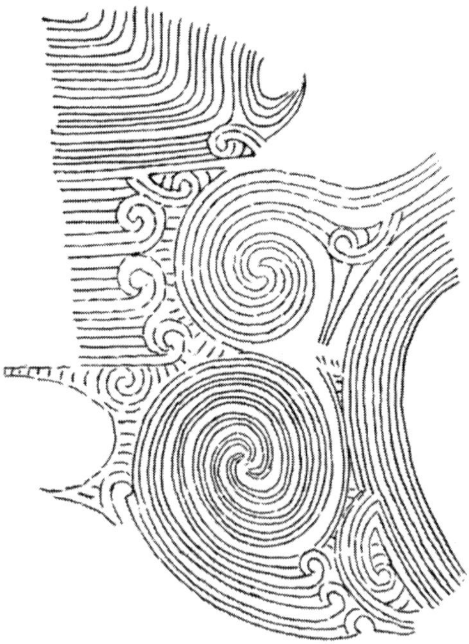

FIG. 77.—Spiral on right cheek.

(*Author's collection.*)

This head is said to have been brought to England prior to 1800.

was likely to be in the way was carefully plucked out and the skin smoothed. I may note here that the untattooed face is called "tapai." Tattooing made the face rough with its cuts, especially when the old bone instruments were used, the later iron instruments having less effect in this respect.

A complete fresco of elaborated moko was a production, we have been told, only of time; and many sittings to the artist and often at long intervals were necessary to develop the pattern fully. Months and even years passed in giving the artist or a successor full scope in the completion of his human pictures. "The worst pain of all," says De Rienzi, "was caused by the incisions on the lips, the corners of the eyes, and the parting of the nostrils." Some idea of the suffering inflicted may be gathered from the fact that nourishment could be taken for a time only through special feeding

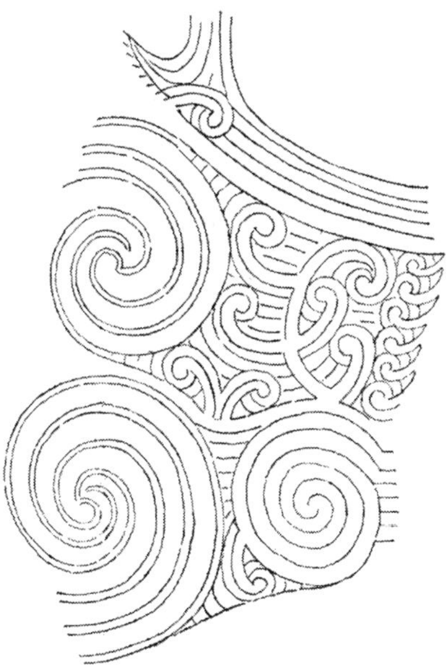

FIG. 78.—Near left ear; good work.

tubes; there are several specimens carved for chiefs in the British Museum. I shall refer later on to the characteristic songs sung to the sufferer in his torments while receiving an allowance of moko,

Lieut.-Col.. Godfrey Munday (*Our Antipodes*, 1852, ii. 154) remarks: "There are even in these islands some fat or jovial faces that this savage operation fails to invest with ferocity."

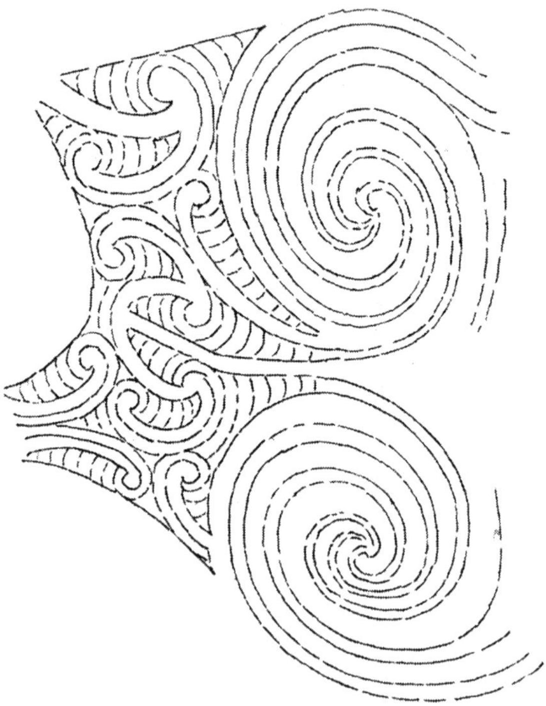

Fig. 79.—Near right ear.
(*Author's collection.*)

The fancy and taste of the artist in moko found ample scope in the exactitude of the lines he cut in the face, and in the variety of his ornamental and figurative designs. He traced out the lines of his intended incisions with charcoal, the marks of which were soon effaced by the streams of blood flowing from his incisions. This result led him sometimes to mark his pattern by scratches with some sharp instrument as a guide to his chisel; the patient in the old days with the aid of a gourd of water as a mirror could view the intended scheme of work, and approve the pattern thus traced

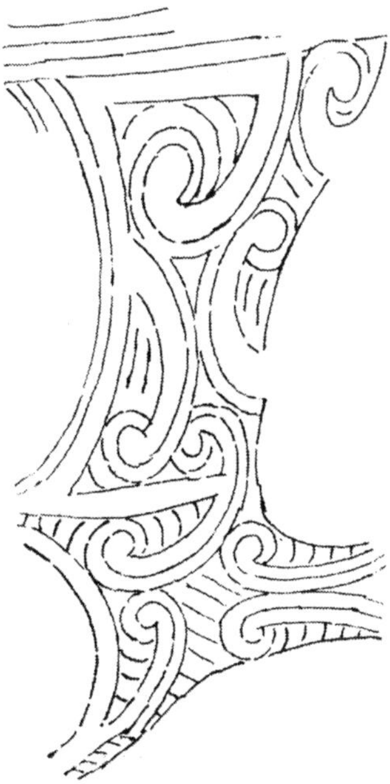

FIG. 80.—Near left ear.
(*Author's collection.*)

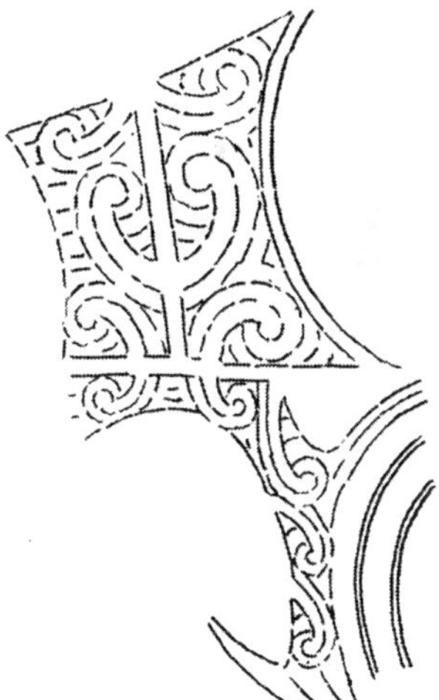

FIG. 81.—Marking near right ear.
(*Author's collection.*)

before it was seriously begun. There was no rubbing out afterwards, though the lines were sometimes deepened by subsequent retouching.

An illustration will enable the reader to realise this. A dried head at Florence is a good example of a "scratched-in" pattern.

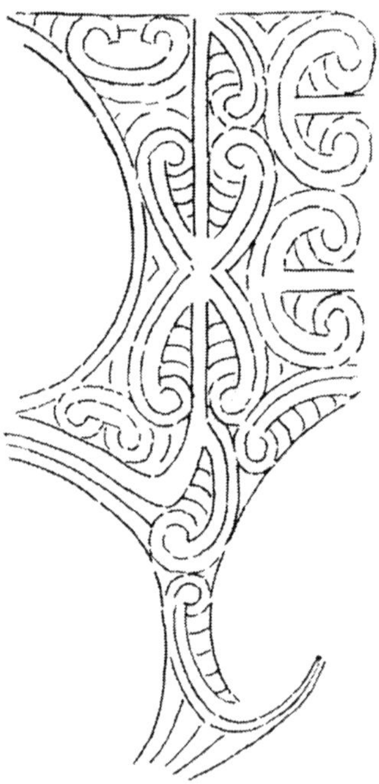

Fig 82.—Near left ear.
(*From Author's collection.*)

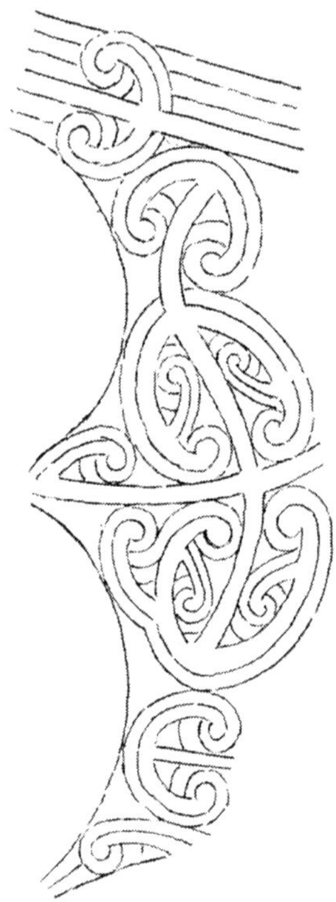

Fig. 83.—Near left ear.

The chisel covered so small a space at each incision that the flow of blood frequently washed out the merely painted pattern. The cast of the face of a Rotorua native (Fig. 98) shows how in his case two to three inches at a time were incised. When finished the well-mokoed face was covered with spiral scrolls, circles, and curved

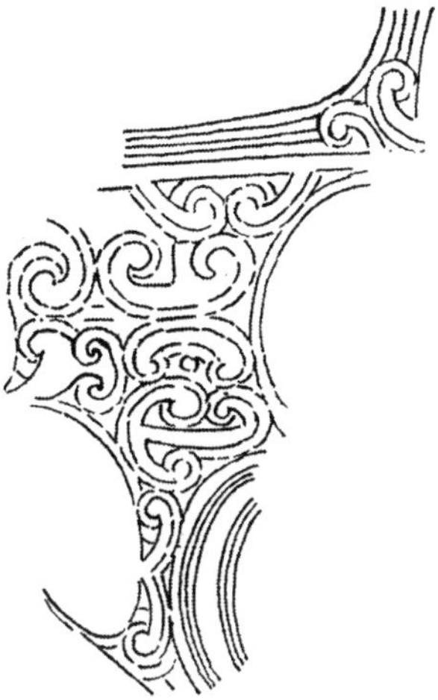

Fig. 84.—Marking near right ear.
(*British Museum.*)

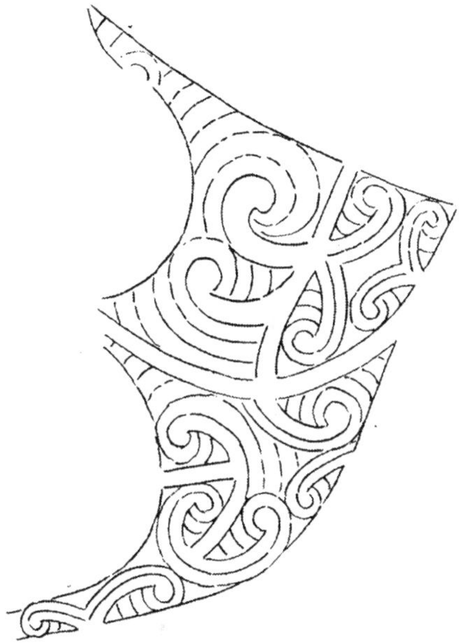

Fig. 85.—Near left ear.
(*Auckland Museum.*)

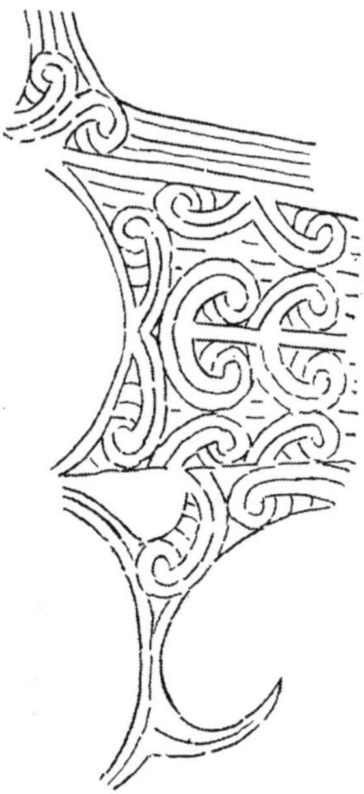

Fig. 86.—Near left ear.
(*Author's collection.*)

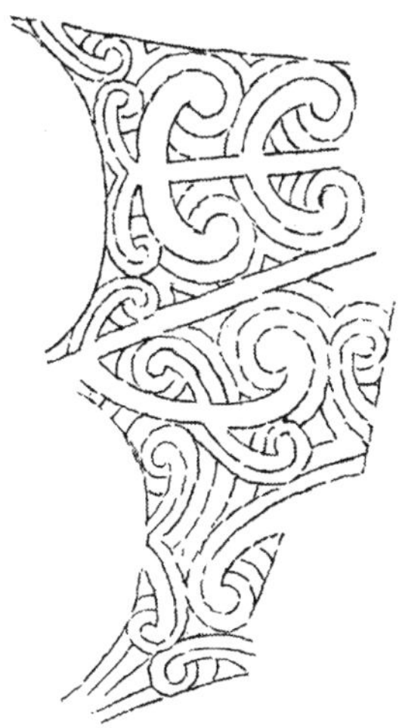

Fig. 87.—Near left ear.

lines; and it is remarkable that, though a certain order is observed and the positions of the principal marks are the same, no two

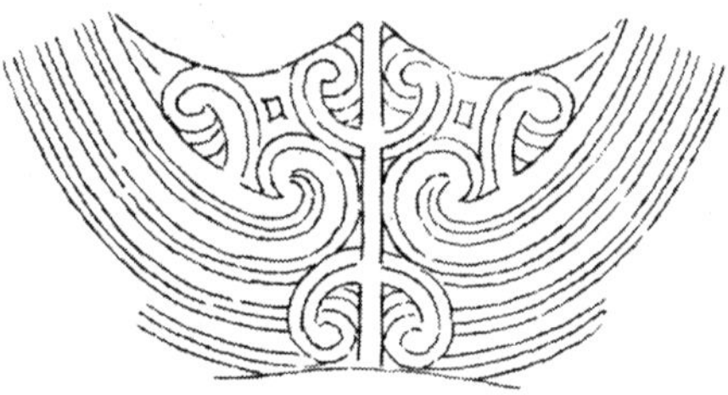

Fig. 88.—Chin patterns.

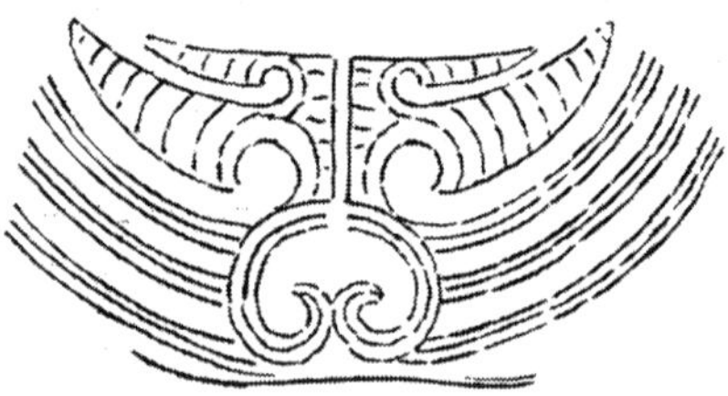

Fig. 89.—Chin patterns.

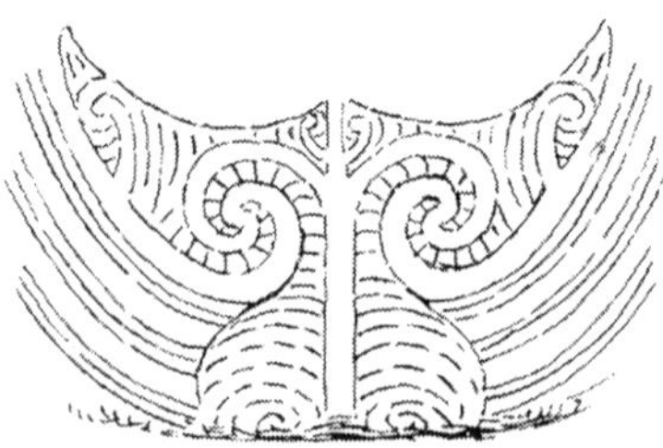

Fig. 90.—Chin patterns.

personages are mokoed alike, the artist being able to produce an infinite variety with the materials at his command. One has only to note the position of the lines and curves of the cuttings in the

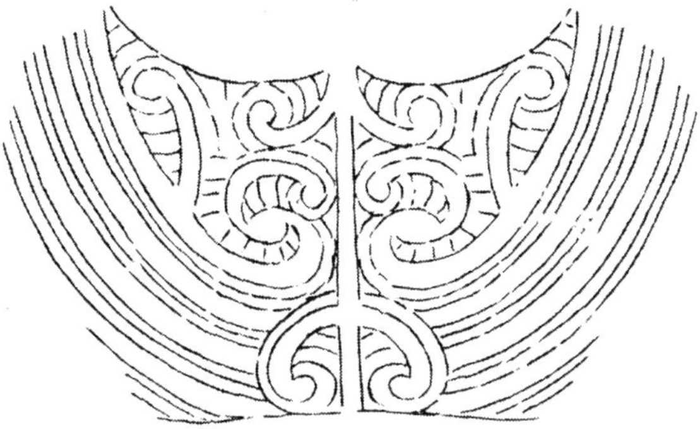

FIG. 91.—A chin pattern.

(*From collection of Prof. Giglioli in Florence. Work done with the old bone instruments.*)

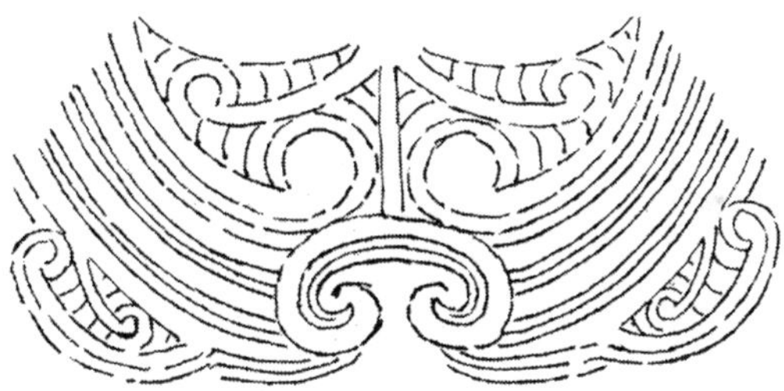

FIG. 92.—Chin.

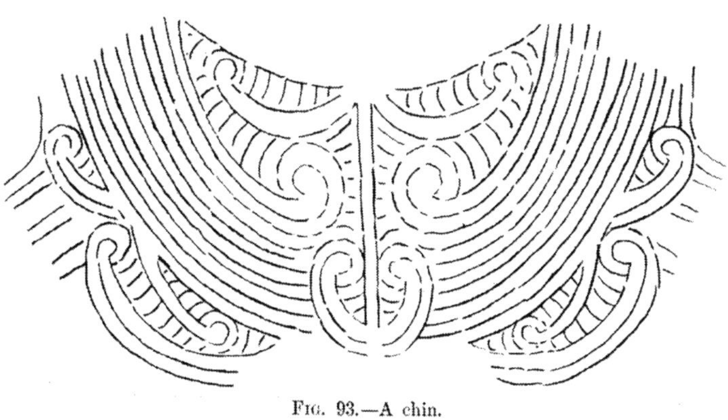

FIG. 93.—A chin.

(*Author's collection; from a fully tattooed head.*)

flesh to see how nearly some take the direction which wrinkles would take; how they follow and emphasise the natural lines of the

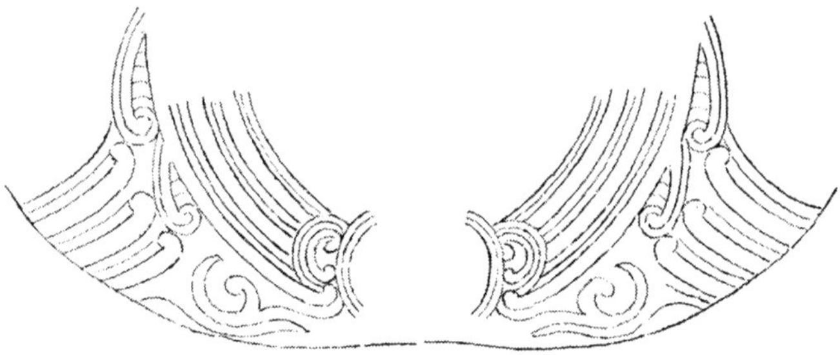

Fig. 94.—Chin.
(*British Museum.*)

face and features with their depressions and projections. The natural lines which time gives on the forehead, the corners of the eyes, and near the muscles seem to give directions for the grooves.

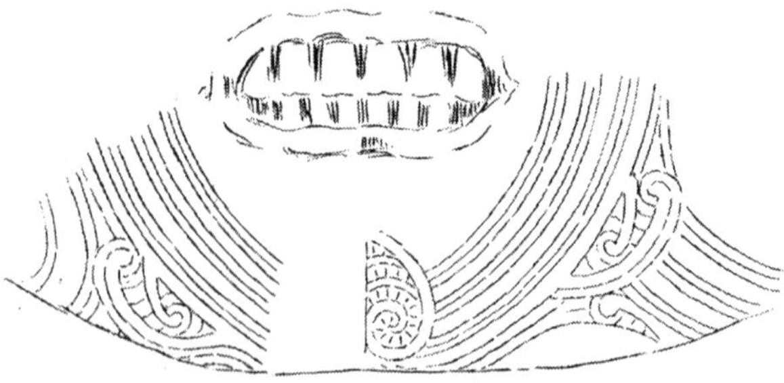

Fig. 95.—An unfinished chin.
(*From Author's collection.*)

The curved pattern on cheeks is the most common. Captain Chegwyn, R.N., who was in H.M.S. *Buffalo* at the Bay of Islands getting spars in 1838–9, notes in his journal that when a chief adopted a son the latter would in due time wear the pattern of moko with which the adoptive father was decorated.

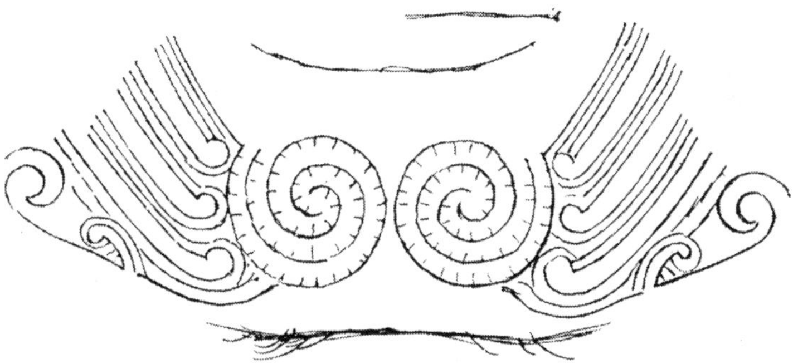

FIG. 96.—Chin.
(*Author's collection.*)

The art of wood-carving was carried to great perfection by the Maori, the gates of their pas, their houses, weapons, canoes, &c., were artistically embellished. The effigies of deified ancestors

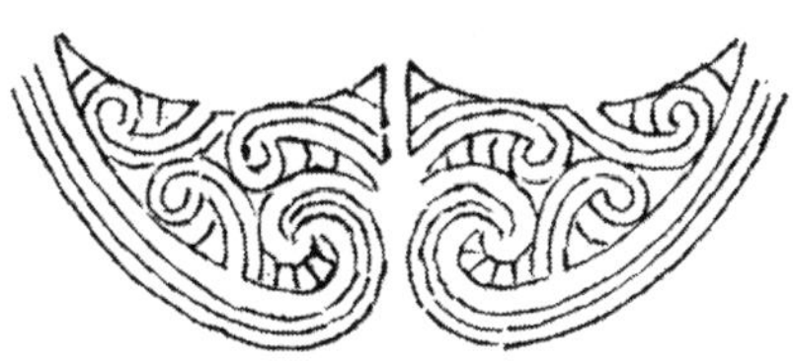

FIG. 97.—Chin.

were thus decorated with their peculiar moko, and extraordinary skill was lavished on them, as Mr. Kerry-Nichols says: "In fact it is the wonderful blending of the circle and sweeping curve which adds to the carving of this ingenious race its special and most attractive charm, and places it beyond that of any other

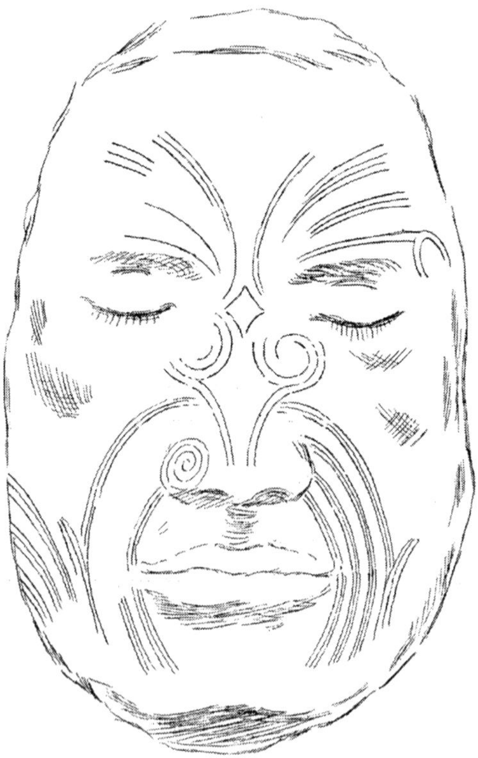

Fig. 98.—Plaster cast of a Rotorua native, 1854.
(Presented to the British Museum by Sir George Grey. Pattern only partly chiselled.)

savage people for beauty, combined with an unique and graceful simplicity."

Dr. Ferdinand von Hochstetter (1866) also remarks on the

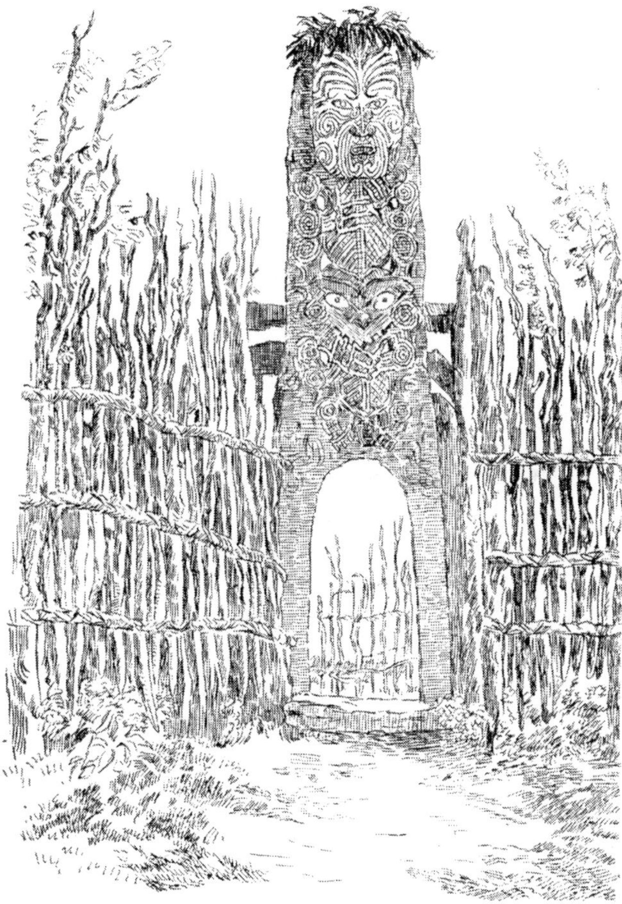

FIG. 99.—Gateway of a Pa, showing a carved head.

(From a drawing on the spot by the Author.)

carved wooden figures met with on the road to the restorative baths of Rotorua. These figures are set up to commemorate the

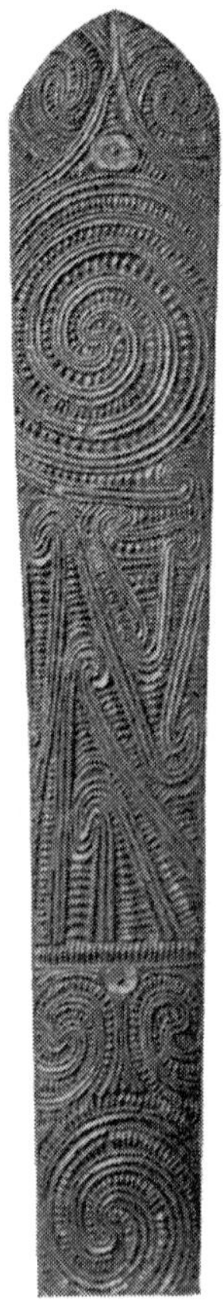

Fig. 100.—End of a staff, showing pattern of thigh tattooing.
(*Leipsic Museum.*)

chiefs who succumbed to their ills; and the remarkable feature of the decoration is the close imitation they show of the tattooing of the deceased, constituting a method of identification that rendered an inscription unnecessary. I have reproduced several

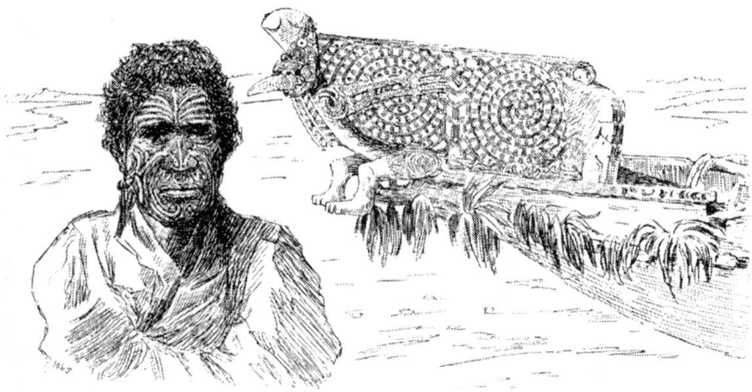

FIG. 101.—A Maori and the prow of war canoe; both showing fine carving.
(*From a drawing by the Author.*)

of these designs, including some in European museums taken from the wooden effigies of past generations, and showing many

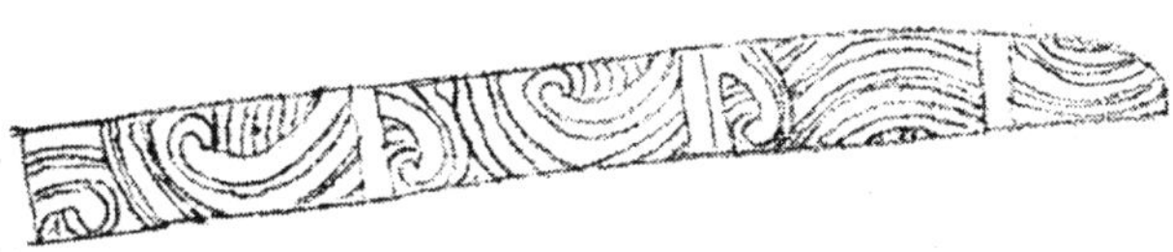

FIG. 102.—Tattooing on a bone.

varieties of moko; for no two Maoris were alike in all their markings. In many parts of the world has tattoo been used;

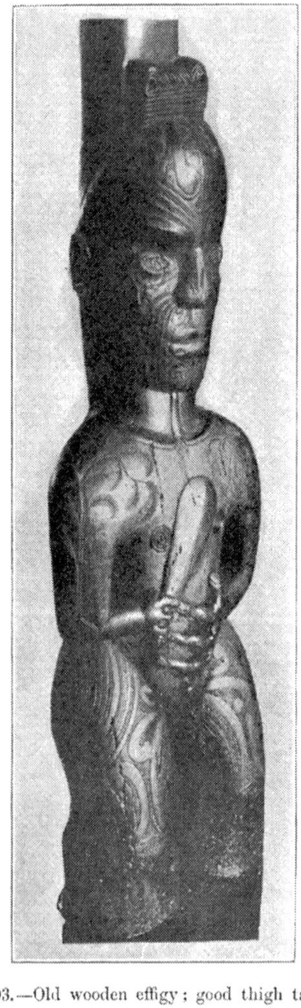

Fig. 103.—Old wooden effigy; good thigh tattooing.

but nowhere was it so boldly perfect as in old New Zealand times. We mentioned one use during the early intercourse of the settlers with the Maoris—viz., the pictures of tattooed faces, or signatures by its pattern or a portion of it, were sometimes

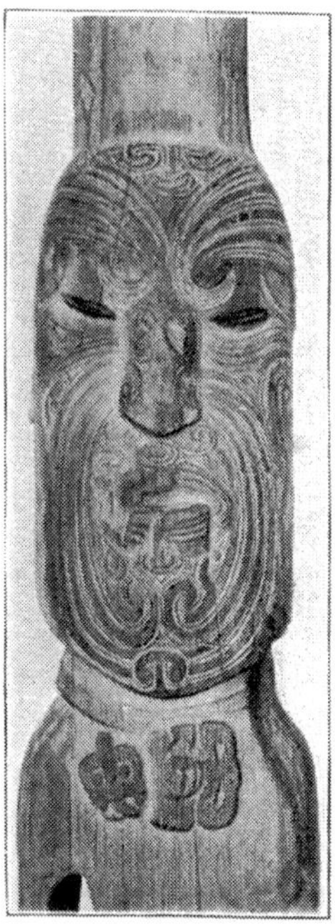

FIG. 104.—Old wooden carving, probably part of a central post in a house at Hawke's Bay, N.Z.

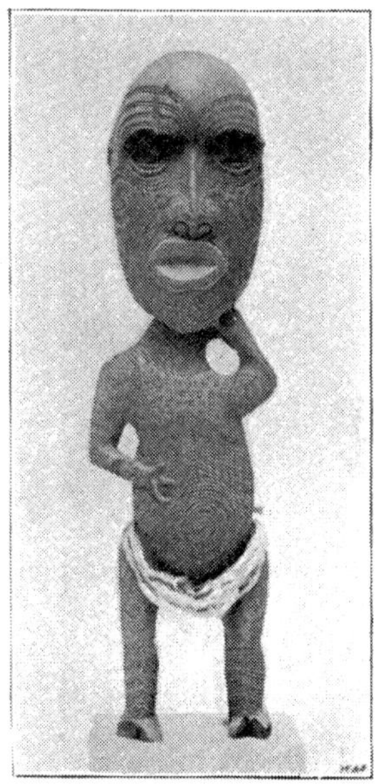

FIG. 105.—An old effigy showing body carving.

(*British Museum.*)

reproduced in deeds evidencing the purchase of lands as they could not write. One instance of moko on a wooden figure is copied in many books and is a real artistic *tour de force*—namely, the bust

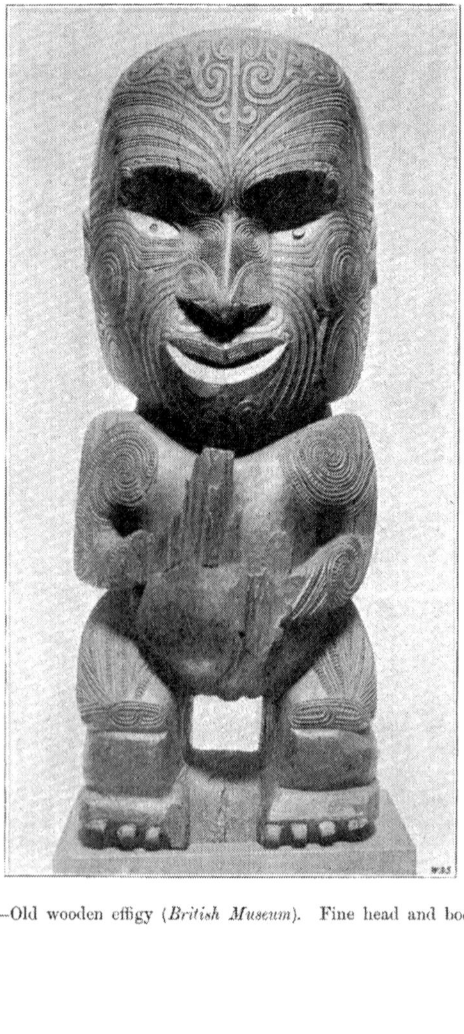

Fig. 106.—Old wooden effigy (*British Museum*). Fine head and body carving.

of himself, by the chief Hongi, who with another tattooed chief Waikato visited England in 1820, and was presented to King George IV. at Mr. Marsden's request. It was in hard wood, done with a rude iron instrument which he fashioned from a piece of old

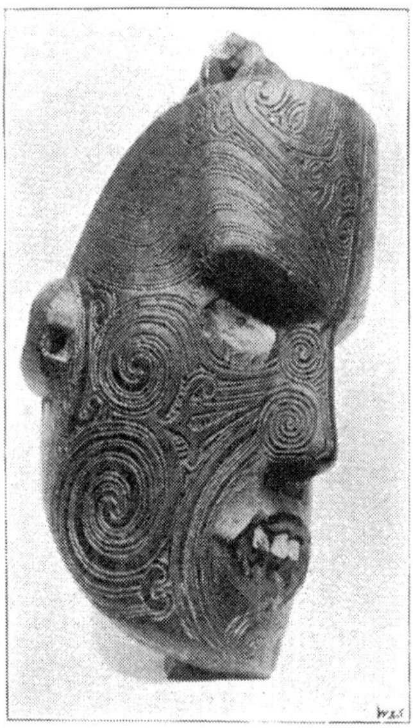

Fig. 107.—Warning figure against trespass on tapued land.

(*British Museum.*)

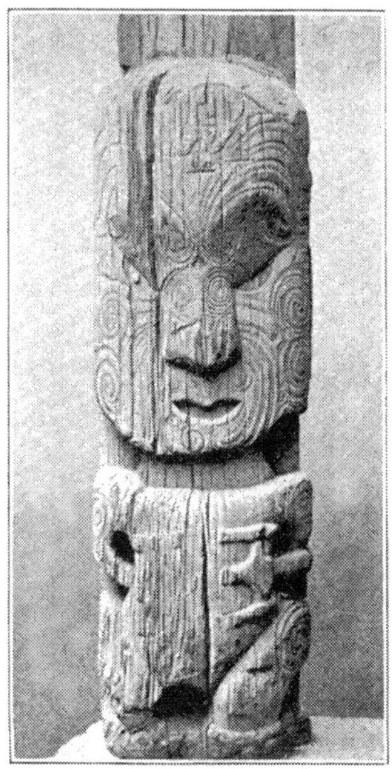

Fig. 108.—Very old effigy; fine head.

hoop-iron; and on it he delineated his own moko. This was in 1816, and it was sent to the Church Mission House, and was a very creditable performance.

The Maori carver at the end of the nineteenth century still

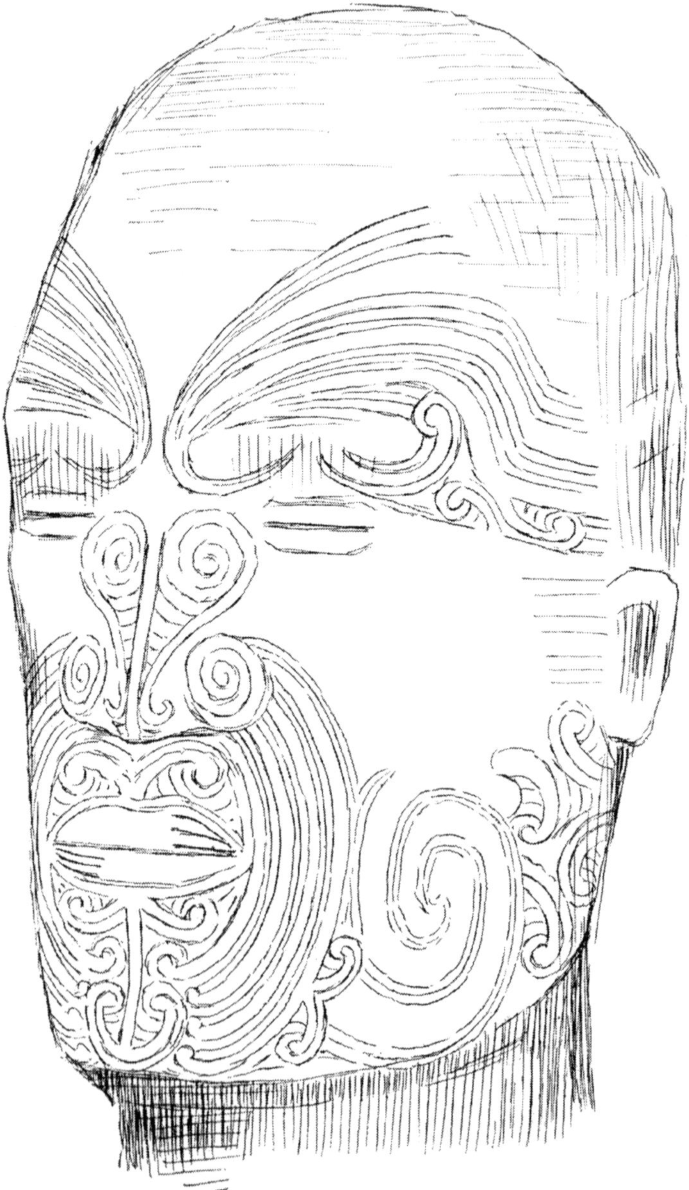

Fig. 109.—Wooden effigy of an ancestor.

(*British Museum.*)

copies and perpetuates the old patterns on wood, and on clumsily shaped heads hewn from blocks of Kauri gum. There is a good specimen in the British Museum presented by Sir Augustus Franks.

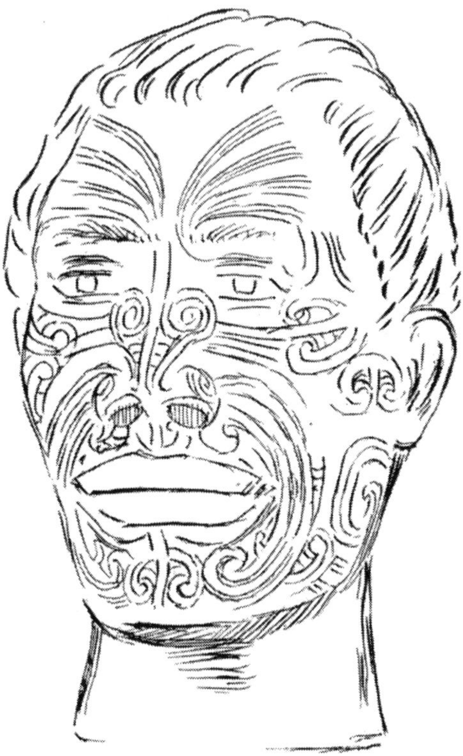

FIG. 110.—A block of Kauri gum, carved as a head.
(Presented to British Museum by Sir Augustus Franks, K.C.B.)

CHAPTER VI

OPERATORS OR ARTISTS

THE operators in moko were generally professional artists who worked for hire, and their different degrees of excellence were as well known as that of painters among the moderns; and they were in fact regarded by their less able countrymen as men of great talent and repute. Skill, of course, came with practice; but even the early efforts of a beginner were in the minds of some Maoris better than no moko at all; and budding artists acquired their craft by practice on those who could not afford to pay for the skilled hand. Variety of excellence naturally showed itself; and the expert was a person held in high esteem. To secure the services of a distinguished operator who was not itinerant, men would go considerable distances. If the operator suspected that he would not be properly remunerated, his work became careless; and there is little doubt that some of the coarser specimens of moko were due to some such cause. On the other hand, presents and payments flowed into the coffers of the man of talent from all quarters, according to the means and ability of the givers. Double-barrelled guns, canoes, clothes, and even slaves have been presented to these distinguished persons as marks of esteem in which their talents were held.

A certain Aranghie was one of the most famous of all artists in moko. There is a portrait of him, drawn by Mr. Earle, who was draughtsman to H.M. surveying ship *Beagle* in 1827. Mr. Earle's remarks on this distinguished artist must be quoted:

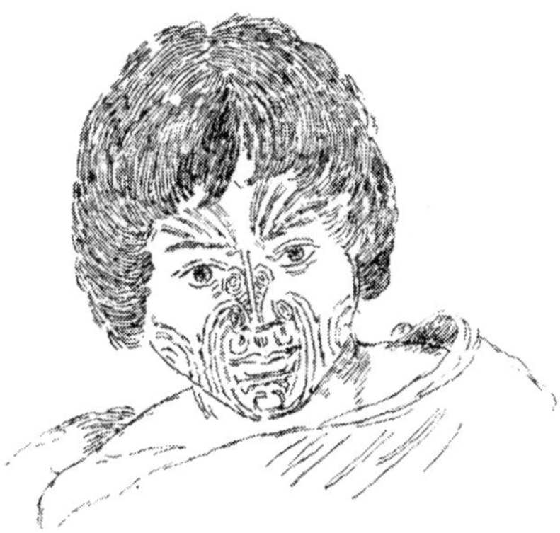

FIG. 111.—Aranghie; a portrait after Earle.

"This professor was considered by his countrymen a perfect master in the art of tattooing, and men of the highest rank and importance were in the habit of travelling long journeys in order to put their skins under his skilful hands. Indeed, so highly were his works esteemed that I have seen many of his drawings exhibited even after his death. A neighbour of mine very lately killed a chief who had been tattooed by Aranghie, and appreciating the artist's work so highly, he skinned the chieftain's thighs, and covered his cartouch-box with it. I was astonished to see with what boldness and precision Aranghie drew his designs on the skin and what beautiful ornaments he produced. No rule and compasses could be more exact than the lines and circles he formed. So unrivalled was he in his profession that a highly finished face of a chief from the hands of this artist is as greatly prized in New Zealand as a head from the hands of Sir Thomas Lawrence is amongst us. It was most gratifying to behold the respect these savages pay to the fine arts. This professor was merely a kooky or slave, but by skill and industry he raised himself to an equality with the greatest men of the country, and as every chief who employed him always made him some handsome present he soon became a man of wealth and was constantly surrounded by important personages. . . . . . My friend Shulitea (King George) sent him every day the choicest things from his own table. Though thus basking in the full sunshine of court favour, Aranghie, like a true genius, was not puffed up with pride by his success, for he condescended to come and take tea with me almost every evening. He was delighted with my drawings, particularly with a portrait I made of him. He copied so well, and seemed to enter with such interest into the few lessons of painting I gave him, that if I were returning from here direct to England I should certainly bring him with me, as I look upon him as a great natural genius."

And there is yet another sketch by a competent observer of the life of another artist in moko, who was kept in constant and profitable employment. Mr. E. J. Wakefield, in his *Adventure in New Zealand*, 1839–44, describes one in the train of a chief who came from the country near East Cape: "Everybody, from the renowned warrior to the girl of twelve years old, crowded to be ornamented by his skilful chisel; shirts, mats, axes, and other articles accumulated in the carver's kit. He was a superior man in many respects. He used to beat everybody at draughts, and had a store of old legends to amuse his audience."

CHAPTER VII

MOKOED EUROPEANS AND MOKOED VISITORS TO EUROPE

RUTHERFORD was himself a remarkable instance of moko and has also so much to say on the subject that I think my readers will be sufficiently interested to hear the conclusion of his history. He was married to the two daughters of his chief, but escaped in 1826 (January 9th), after nearly ten years' captivity. He had been sent off by the natives on the mission of decoying an American brig nearer to the shore. As soon as the captain of the vessel saw him he exclaimed, "Here is a white New Zealander," and on hearing his story took him off.

After his return to England he occasionally maintained himself by accompanying a travelling caravan of wonders, showing his tattooing and telling portions of his extraordinary adventures. In 1829 he was exhibited in London. The publication of his adventures gave him much gratification, as did the painting of his portrait, though he suffered much inconvenience from sitting to the artist in frosty weather with the upper part of his body undraped. He disliked being "shown" for money, but submitted to it in order that with the sum he obtained for his manuscript he might return to Otaheite. His journal of his ten years' imprisonment in New Zealand tells us of the five other fellow prisoners, who were tattooed with him in 1816. They were separated; he saw one of them fall a victim owing to ignorance of native customs. Rutherford records a meeting with a well-tattooed Englishman, who had been

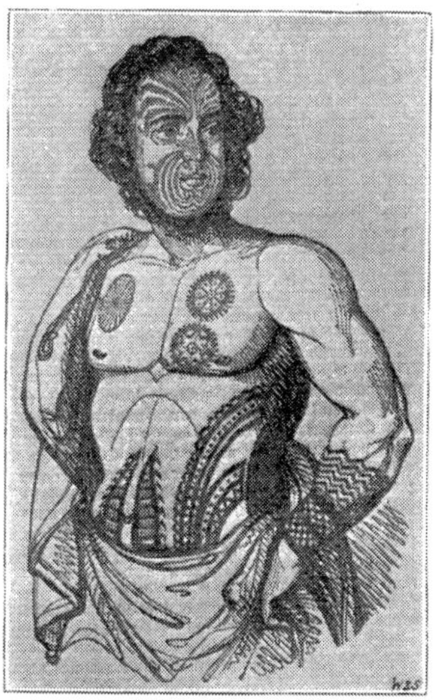

FIG. 112.—Portrait of John Rutherford.
(From an original drawing taken in 1828.)

about eight years in the country, twenty-four years of age, and enjoying the rank of a chief. Rutherford kept his intention of looking out for a ship to escape a secret from this man, for he was too much attached to the natives to be trusted.

Rutherford and his companions are by no means the only white men who have been mokoed. George Bruce, the first of the early Europeans so treated in New Zealand, about the year 1806, acquired a good knowledge of the language and customs. He became a chief, married the daughter of a chief Te Pahi, and resided near the Bay of Islands. He exercised a good influence on the people. Later he was badly treated by an unprincipled skipper, who got him and his wife on board ship, landed him at Malacca, and sold the wife to another captain at Penang. Through the influence of the Governor of Penang his wife was restored; but neither were heard of after a stay in Bengal, and they never returned to the Bay of Islands.

In 1807 a vessel called the *Sydney Cove* landed in New Zealand a gang of men for the seal-fishery in the South. All were killed and eaten, except a lad, James Caddell, who in the massacre touched the mat of a chief Tako, and was preserved by reason of its sanctity. Caddell gradually adopted the manners and customs of the tribe. The *Sydney Gazette* for April 3rd, 1823, states that nine years before he was married to a chief's daughter, the sister of a chief. Caddell soon became transformed from the English sailor boy to the terrifying New Zealand chief; he was tattooed and became a noble. After much persuasion he was induced to visit New South Wales, and even then he would not go without his partner, to whom he was tenderly attached. He was about thirty, and for some days they paraded the streets of Sydney in Maori costume. They returned by the first opportunity.

Earle, too, mentions some runaway convicts, who became slaves in New Zealand, and who were tattooed. He says that in 1827 the brig *Wellington* was seized by convicts *en route* to

Norfolk Island. At the Bay of Islands the outlaws who landed at Kororarika were seized by the natives and put on board ships with the exception of six. Earle says he saw them in the suite of one of the chiefs: "I chanced to be in the house alone, and was amazed by seeing an Englishman enter the hut with his face tattooed all over. Not being aware he was one of the runaways from the *Wellington*, I spoke to him. He slunk into our cooking-house on pretence of lighting his pipe, and before ten minutes had elapsed the house was in flames."

Thomson says one unemployed white man (Pakeha Maori), who was tattooed, visited England and acted the part of a New Zealand savage in several provincial theatres. He married an Englishwoman, who accompanied him to New Zealand; but she eloped with a Yankee sailor, because the tattooed actor's former Maori wife met him and obtained over him an influence the white woman could not combat. Lieutenant-Colonel Munday (1847) mentions some smacks belonging to the Maoris. In one little cutter the master was an aboriginal, and the crew of one man was a Pakeha Maori or "white man blackwashed." Lieutenant-Colonel Munday adds that he was informed the man was tattooed and married to a Maori woman.

Sydney, New South Wales, was the scene of the earliest mokoed visitors from New Zealand. The first in England was one Moyhanger in 1805, a native, who arrived with Mr. Savage, author of *Some Account of New Zealand*, published in London, 1807. In 1807 Matara (by name) arrived; and in 1809 in the whaler *Argo* came Ruatara, aged 18, with two others all tattooed. Ruatara was son of the chief who was father-in-law to Bruce, the mokoed white man. As the Maoris made good sailors many worked well on ships; others travelled with missionaries. In 1818 the chiefs Te Teri and Tui, who had but little moko, were in England; and many others since.

In 1820 came the cruel Hongi, eater of men, with another

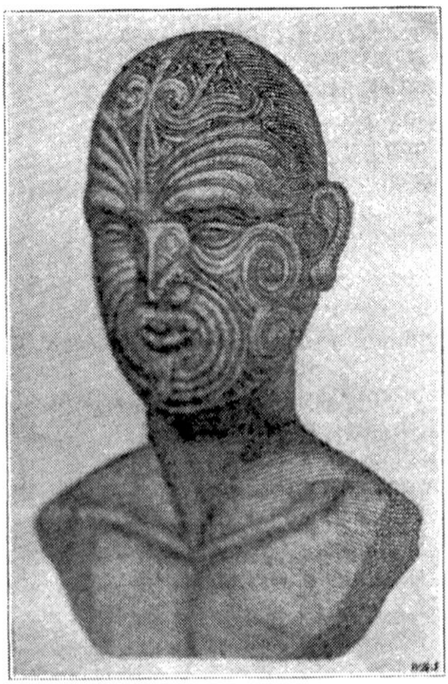

FIG. 113.—A bust of himself in wood by Hongi.

chief Waikato. They were spoken of in England as Christian converts. Their visit to Cambridge led to the translation of the Bible into the Maori language. From their pronunciation Professor Lee reduced their language into a written one, and composed a grammar and dictionary; and this afforded a means of translating the Bible and Prayer-book into their native language; and the demand for these books gradually increased. Of course many words had to be coined into the native pronunciation, and manufactured words were introduced into this hybrid language. Coined words had to be written according to the Maori pronunciation that most nearly approached the words. Thus, Scriptures became Karipitura, Bible Paipera, Pharisee Parihi, Israel Iharaira, Sabbath Hapati, Phylacteries Pairakere, and so on.

Of course "tattooing" still remained moko. It is narrated that much public interest was aroused in these chiefs, and their finely tattooed faces excited general attention. George IV. gave them an audience. Hongi's bearing was dignified when treated as a great man, but when regarded merely as an object of curiosity he never failed to show his disgust and even indignation. On this subject the Rev. Mr. Taylor gives the following narration: "A striking instance of this occurred in a gentleman's house, where a large party had been invited to meet the chief; Hongi had assumed all the airs of a superior, and acted the prince which he knew well how to do; until he observed some ladies evidently tracing the lines on his tattooed face, whilst a smile played on their own, which he thought implied a feeling of pity towards himself; immediately he rose in a state of great excitement, threw himself across three chairs, and covering his face with his hands, remained in that position until the company left."

These two chiefs had no sooner returned to New Zealand with Missionary Kendal, than Hongi armed his whole tribe and its allies with the muskets obtained in England; and throwing aside the mask of religion (not that of moko, of course) he pursued the career of a bloodthirsty warrior. Owing to him the whole population of the North Island was thinned and scattered, and that of the Middle Island almost destroyed. In 1826 the

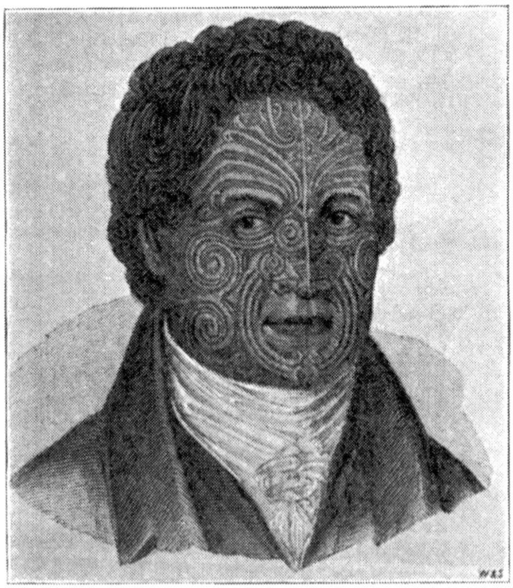

FIG. 114.—Portrait of Te Pehi Kupe.
(*From a sketch by Mr. J. Sylvester, of Liverpool.*)

Southern Chief Pehi (mentioned before) resolved to emulate Hongi and visit England with a view to procuring arms wherewith to revenge himself. A whaling vessel came into Cook's Straits. Pehi immediately went on board, bidding his followers paddle back to shore and leave him on the ship. His visit to England, which has been recounted in another chapter, was unsuccessful so far as obtaining arms was concerned. The crowds who followed Te Pehi in the streets of Liverpool led an English showman to bring two tattooed New Zealanders to England as a commercial speculation. In 1830 they were exhibited in different parts of the country. Both acknowledged they had partaken of human flesh. The elder of the two had a small part of his left cheek untouched with tattooing. They were at Derby in March 1830, fell ill of measles, and were abandoned; they were however maintained by a gentleman of that town until they recovered.

A chief, whose moko signature appears in this book, É Gnoni, was also in this country.

A partly tattooed Maori sailor died, 1849, at Guy's Hospital.

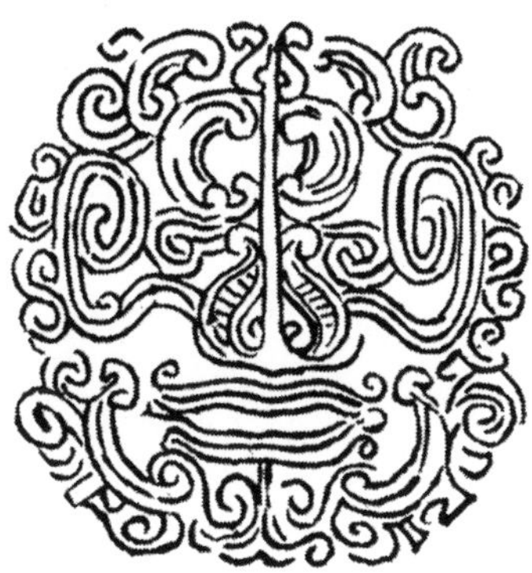

FIG. 115.—É Gnoni a chief of Mukou (Lat. 38 deg. S). Once resident in London. Drawn by himself on the wood.

(*Tracing by the Author.*)

In 1855, the Chief John Williams Hipango, from the Wanganui district, reached London *viâ* Sydney. During his stay a vessel arrived in port which had been recovered from its mutinous crew by eight New Zealand sailors who were on board. These natives were sent to the Sailors' Home, and heard in chapel the first service ever given in the Maori language in

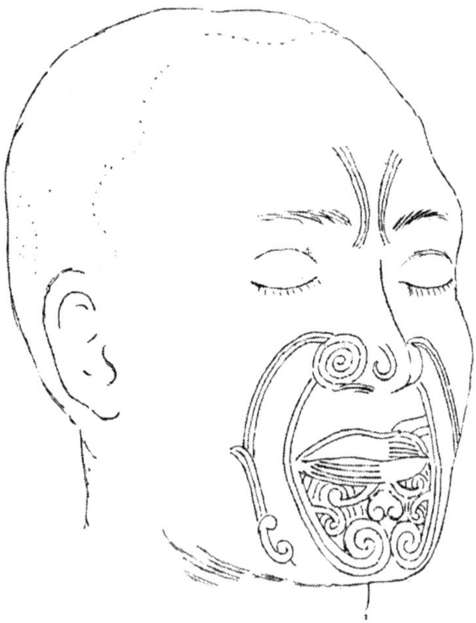

FIG. 116.—Wax model of a Maori who died in Guy's Hospital, London.
(*From a sketch by the Author.*)

London. Hipango visited his countrymen, of whom several were baptised. He was received in a private audience by Her Majesty and H.R.H. The Prince Consort on the occasion of delivering presents sent from New Zealand.

Dr. Karl Scherzer's narrative of the voyage of the Austrian frigate *Novara* in 1859 mentions that two mokoed Waikatos, named Wiremu Toetoe and Hemara Rerehau Paraone, joined the ship's company of their own will. When the ship left Auckland somewhat later a boat with several natives came alongside; and the Vicar-General, anxious that Protestant natives should not alone be shipped to Europe, was found to have brought some wonderfully tattooed Roman Catholic natives to accompany the vessel. But it was too late, for she was already in motion; and the Vicar-General, a warm-hearted Irishman, had to return with his *protégés*, his praiseworthy object being unaccomplished. At Vienna the two natives visited their Majesties at the Imperial Palace. After some stay, they were presented (on the recommendation of the Director of the State Printing Office) with some implements that they might avail themselves at home of the knowledge they had acquired. In 1860 they came *viâ* Germany to England, and were presented to the Queen; and ultimately returned to Auckland. In his native land Toetoe issued from the press too stirring publications.

In 1884 the great Ariki, or Chief of Chiefs—namely, King Tawhiao, a pensioner of the New Zealand Government—came to England. His object was to see the Queen, but this was not permitted. He stayed with his suite at Montague Place. Attracted to Mr. Cutter's, in Great Russell Street, by a collection of New Zealand arms, he left this printed visiting card. The author has their signatures in fair writing.

King Tawhiao.
Major Wiremu Te Wheoro
Topia Turoa
Hori Ropihana
Patora Te Tuhi

The major, who was a member of the House of Representatives, was not tattooed.

The white hat Tawhiao often wore in London was a contrast to

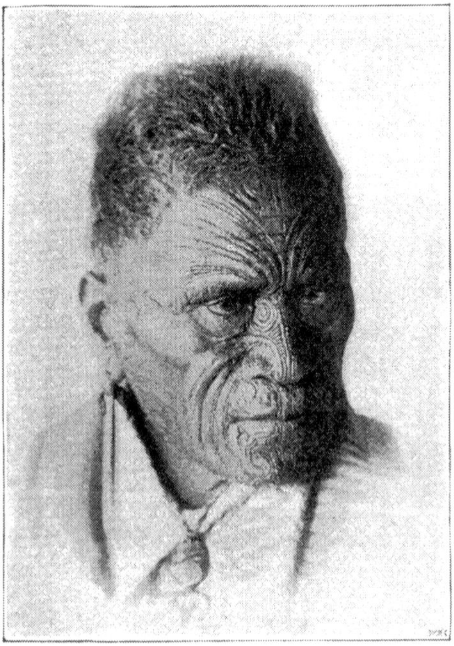

FIG. 117.—King Tawhiao, died August 27, 1894.
(From a photograph.)

his darkened visage, but not in accord with his mokoed face. His body was covered with carving. He said for a fortnight when his lips were being done he had to be fed most tenderly. At the Crystal Palace on the occasion of his visit, there was a special display of fireworks, which included a pyrotechnical representation of his face. Messrs. Brock and Co. used blue lights to represent the tattooing marks, and it was reserved for that celebrated firm of fireworkers to achieve the apotheosis of moko.

CHAPTER VIII

MOKO IN LEGEND AND SONG

In the interesting native mythology in the Rev. Mr. Taylor's book, it is stated that Maui its grand hero is said to have tattooed the lips of the native dog, which accounts for its muzzle being always black, as Kahutara tattooed the face of heaven and made it dark, and also that of man. In White's *Ancient History of the Maori* there is this legend, which serves in some sort as an account of the origin of moko. Tama-nui-a-raki paid a visit to his ancestors; they asked him, "What brought you here?" He answered, "To obtain your services to make on my face the lines I now see marked on yours." Tama's face was marked all over, but when he went to bathe it all washed off, and this took place a second time. He then asked, "I see you are tattooed so that when you wash it does not wash off; but mine is gone as soon as I bathe." They said, "Rise, and go to your other ancestors, Taka (take action), Ha (breath), Tua a Piko (a little awry), Ta Wai Tiri (splashing water), with whom you will find the soot to make the moko permanent." Tama went to his other ancestors, and was asked why he paid the visit. He answered, "To obtain knowledge of the art I see exhibited on your faces." They said, "But it is a very painful operation." He said, "It cannot be death, as you have borne it and live." They said, "But some die under the operation." However on the following day the instruments were got ready, and as soon as Tama had lain down and shut his eyes and the operator had cut some of the lines on his face, he fainted away. On recovering consciousness, he exclaimed:

"O Taka! O Ha
Tua Piko and Ta Whai Tiri
I shall expire.

His ancestors said:

"We do not cause the pain,
It is the instruments
And blood and severed flesh.
Now darkness comes,
Black darkness covers thee;
And He is watchful;
We also are watching now."

Tama again fainted, but on recovering, said:

"O Taka! O Ha!
In agony I shall die."

And again his ancestors said:

"We do not cause the pain,
It is the instruments
And blood and severed flesh,

And darkness comes,
Black darkness covers thee
And He is watchful;
We are watching;
Drink water and be refreshed."

Tama now went and bathed, and said:

"Man near death reels and trembles,
And beloved ones show him affection.'

He then lay down with his face to the earth, and one of the operators kneeled on him to cause the blood to flow from the punctures. Again he fainted away, and was carried to the settlement in a litter. A fire was kindled, and he was laid near to it. After three days he could see things around him, and day after day the moko healed, and he could walk about and go to bathe. Soon he recovered and said to his ancestors: "I will now return home to my children."

From Sir George Grey's book, *Hakiraka O Nga Maori*, I give the tattoo song for a man—"He Whakawai Taanga Moko":—

"E noho ana, e kai-tahi ana,
Ki te titiro, ki nga rewa
I te ihu, O Tutetawha
E wehoki ana, me he peke ngarara
Taia mai ra, ki te uhi Mataora
Taria, e tuku atu,
Ki to wahine, takiri karito kowhara,
Naku, koe i whakanoko. &c., &c,

Which may be translated:

> "We are sitting eating together,
> And are looking at the prints
> Over the eyebrows
> And nose of Tutetawha;
> They are curved like lizards' legs.
> Tattoo him with good points.
>
> "Be not impatient to go
> To the girl who gathers you sweet greens
> In baskets of kowhara.
> Let every line be traced
> On this man who will pay;
> Let the figures be handsome;
> Let our songs lull the pain,
> And inspire thee with fortitude,
> E hiki Tangaroa?
> E hiki Tangoroa?"

And the song when a young woman is being tattooed, which certainly supplies the motive for the operation:

> "Takoto ra, e hine
> Pirori e,
> Kia taia o ngutu,
> Pirore e,
> Mo to haerenga atu, ki nga whare tapere
> I kiia ana mai,
> Ko hea tenei wahine kino?
> E haere mai nei," &c.

Given well is the following from a paper by Mr. W. Colenso in the *Transactions of the New Zealand Institute:*

> "Lay thyself quietly down, oh daughter,
> (Soon it is done,)

That thy lips may be well tattooed;
(’Tis quickly performed.)
For thy going to visit the young men’s houses;
Lest it should be said
Whither indeed is this ugly woman going?
Now coming hitherward.
Keep thyself still, lying down, oh young lady,
(Round the tap goes.)
That thy lips may be well tattooed,
Also thy chin;
That thou mayest be beautiful.
Thus it goes fast.
For thy going to visit the houses of courtship,
Lest it should be said of thee,
Whither does this woman think of going with her red lips?

“Who is walking this way?
(Still it is revolving.)
Give thyself willingly to be tattooed;
Briefly it is over.
For thy going to the house of amusement;
Also thou wilt be spoken of:
‘Whither goes this woman with her bare lips,[1]
Hastening hither, indeed, in that state?’
(Round it revolves.)
It is done. It is tattooed.
(Soon it is indeed.)
Give hither quietly thy chin to be imprinted;
(Nimbly the hand moves.)
For thy going to the houses of the single men,
Lest these ill words be said—
‘Whither goes this woman with her red chin,
Who is coming this way?’”

---

[1] Literally, plain, unadorned, without ornament or covering, applied sneeringly.

The song of the operator says in no uncertain terms that perfect work must be liberally paid for, a proposition from which no artist will dissent.

The operator sings:

"Te tangata i te whakautu,
Kia ata whakanakonako;
Tangata, i te whakautu kore,
Kokoia, kia tatahi,
Patua i te whakatangitangi;
E hiki Tangaroa?
E hiki Tangaroa?"

Which may be rendered:

"He who pays well let him
Be beautifully ornamented,
But he who forgets the operator
Let him be done carelessly.
Be the lines far apart,
E hiki Tangaroa?
E hiki Tangaroa?
Strike that the chisel
As it cuts along may sound.
O Hiki Tangaroa?
Men do not know the skill
Of the operator in driving his
Sounding chisel along,
E hiki Tangaroa?"

This song was chiefly, says the Rev. Mr. Taylor, to remind the gentleman of the duty he owed the operator, who, not having any regular professional charge, chiefly depended on the liberality of his patient, who was expected, not only to feed him with the best, but to make him a handsome present as well. When the operator suspected he would not be remembered he frequently became careless in his work, and rendered the person an object for life; some of the mokos are very coarsely done, whilst others are finished with an artist's touch, by which we may judge the way they severally paid the owner of the sounding chisel.

Again, from Sir George Grey's invaluable collection of Maori songs and legends, the lament of the brother on the death (1846) of the celebrated Te Heuheu has this verse (translated):

> "Turn yet this once thy bold athletic frame,
> And let me see thy skin carved o'er with lines
> Of blue; and let me see thy face,
> So beautifully chiselled into various forms;
> Ah, the people now are comfortless and sad."

CHAPTER IX

THE DECADENCE OF MOKO

WITH regard to the rapid decadence of the art of tattooing, it has been already mentioned that the missionaries long ago discouraged the practice as a mark of heathendom. Yate (1835)

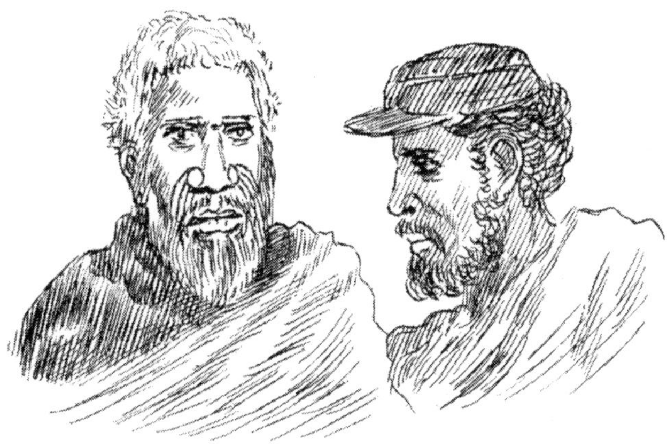

FIG. 118.—Maori father and son, the latter without tattooing. (*Sketch*, 1866.)

says that in all mission stations tattooing has been forbidden, and that it is generally understood that any person coming to live at a mission station must no longer submit himself "to such a savage and debasing performance." Nowadays, the art is no longer practised among the men, and living examples of it are only to be found amongst the older generation. With the death of King Tawhiao on August 27th, 1894, at the age of 70, one of the last really fine specimens of moko was lost to the

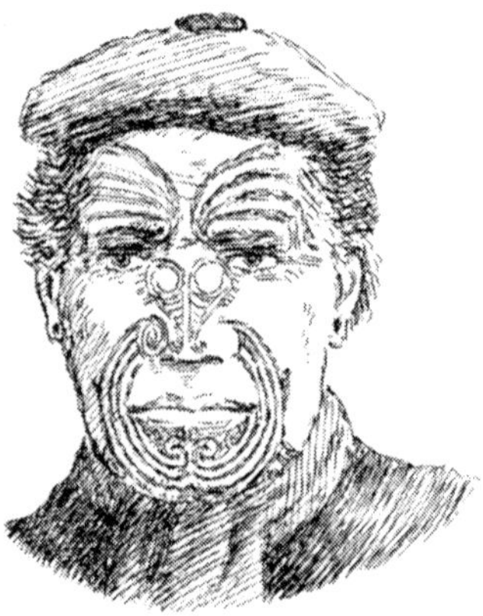

FIG. 119.—Unfinished moko.
(From a sketch from life by the Author, 1866.)

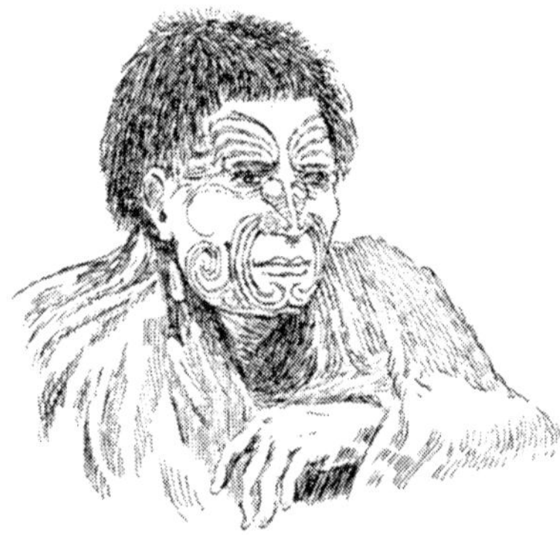

FIG. 120.—Unfinished tattooing.
(From a sketch from life by the Author, 1865.)

world. Though not completely covered with tracery, he might have been any age; for where moko is elaborated time can write no wrinkles. The art will soon have to be studied in the dried Maori heads preserved in many museums and private collections. And since as an art moko is vanishing, I have done my best to write some account of it before its remembrance quite passes away; though I have by no means exhausted this interesting subject and more yet remains to be written on it. As early as 1835, Darwin, in the famous journal of the expedition of H.M.S. *Beagle*, records that the practice of moko was diminishing; but that as it was the badge of distinction between chief and slave, in his opinion it would not probably very soon be disused. Its effect of preventing the usual signs of age from showing themselves in wrinkles has been mentioned, and it should be added that moko has the corresponding result of adding an appearance of premature age to the face of a young person. European civilisation, new wants and order of things, obliterated the distinctions which prevailed, upset all their social order, and reduced the entire race to one dead level of social inferiority in the presence of the Pakeha.

By degrees tattooing went, and now in a short time it will

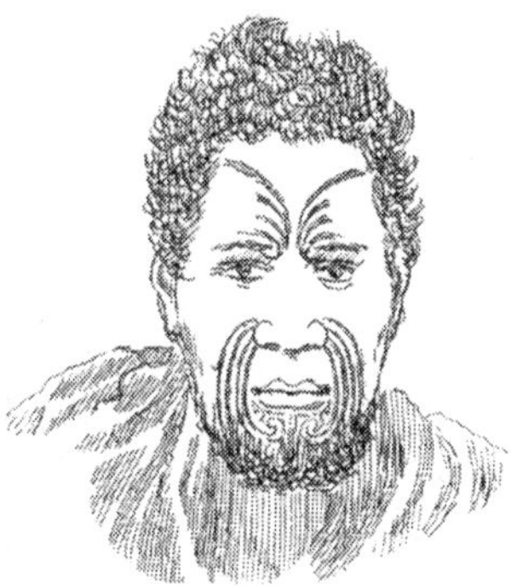

Fig. 121.—Unfinished tattoo.
(*A sketch*, 1866.)

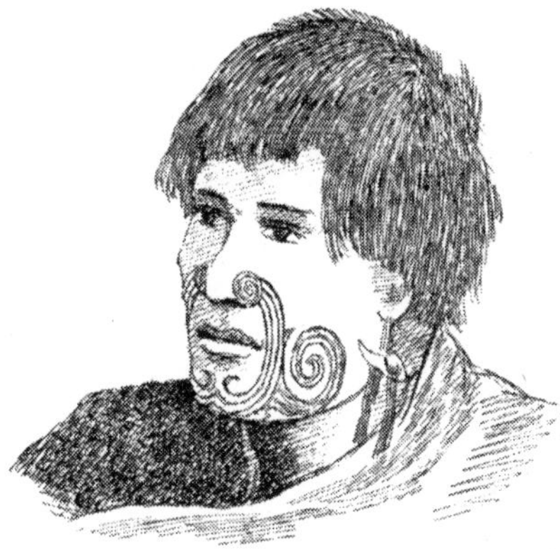

Fig. 122.—Partly tattooed.
(*A sketch*, 1866.)

disappear. I noticed in 1864-66, as I have elsewhere mentioned, that there was the beard and moustache on those whose faces already bore moko, except among the older men. One singular result ensued during the period of transition. Such of the natives as were converted before their moko was complete discontinued the task and remained as they were, moko being incapable of oblitera-

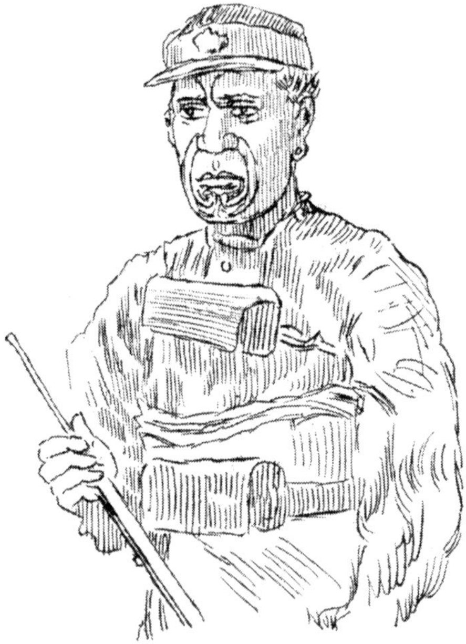

FIG. 123.—Unfinished tattoo.
(*From a sketch by the Author*, 1864.)

tion. The effect is curious, not to say ludicrous, when they appeared partly tattooed and partly plain.

Speaking of the year 1847, the Bishop of Waiapu (the Right Rev. William Williams, D.C.L.) gives an account of an incident which throws some light on the decay of moko. There was a quarrel on the east coast about a native woman, a widow, being married. The discontented party fired a gun and gave notice that tattooing should be revived for the purpose of annoying the members of the church, and a young man was that morning submitted to the operation. And tattooing continued daily for some weeks. So strong was the inclination of the young people to be made like their elders in appearance that very many went off to receive their moko in spite of the opposition of their friends; the Christian party made a determined effort to dissuade their relations,

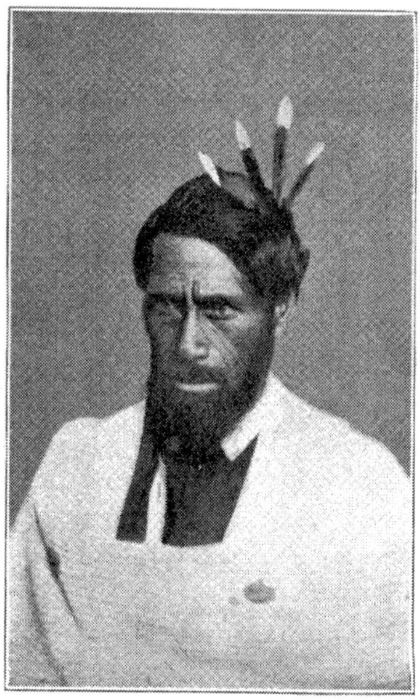

FIG. 124.—Photograph of Maori wearing hair over tattoo.

and subsequently refused to hold intercourse with them when their efforts had proved fruitless. This state of things went on for more than six months, when a reconciliation took place.

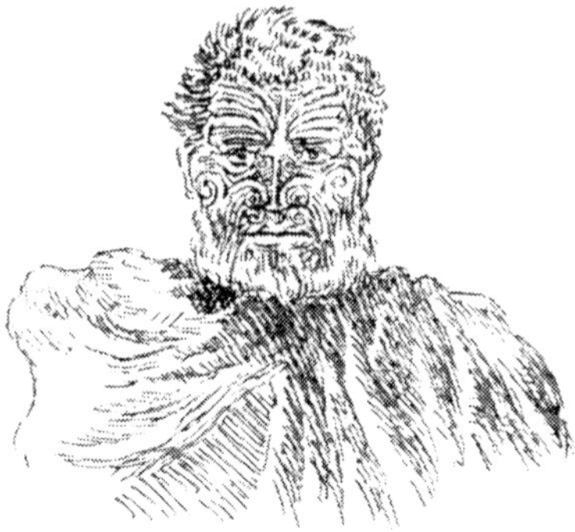

Fig. 125.—Old man wearing hair over tattoo
(*From life by the Author*, 1865.)

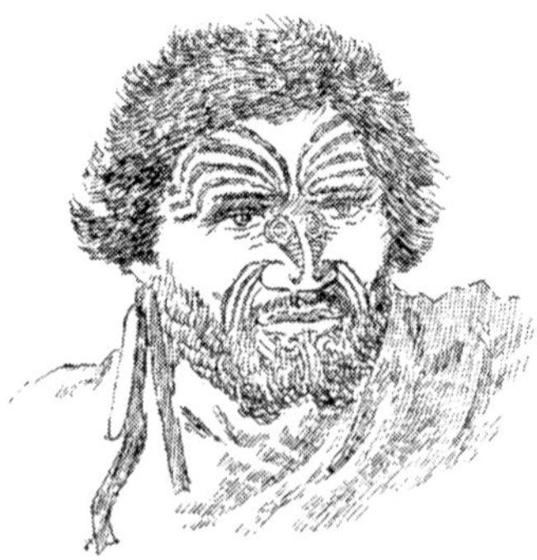

Fig. 126.—Incomplete tattoo, hair grown over markings.
(*From a sketch from life by the Author.*)

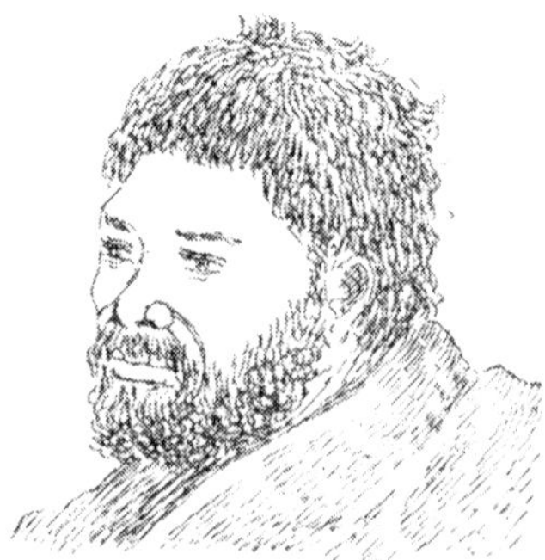

Fig. 127.—Slight tattooing with hair
(*Sketch by Author*, 1864.)

Photography came into use just in time for the recorder of moko. The deeper cut patterns come out best; for "chiselled" moko makes thick and deep lines on the flesh, leaving scars which photograph well, while the lightly traced marks do not appear so distinctly. One often notices that a photographer has inked in the lines, a magnifying glass shows where he has failed to follow them accurately; or one sees the native just touched up with the brush to give the requisite strength and make the pattern come out well. These are generally a little incorrect. I took many portraits

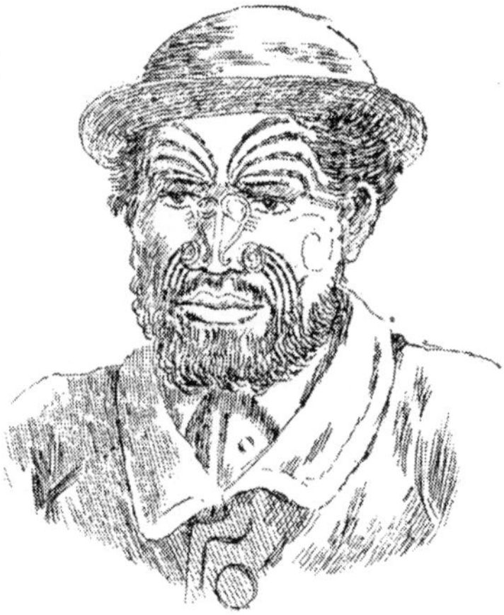

FIG. 128.—A Maori sailor (1865).
(*Sketch from life by Author.*)

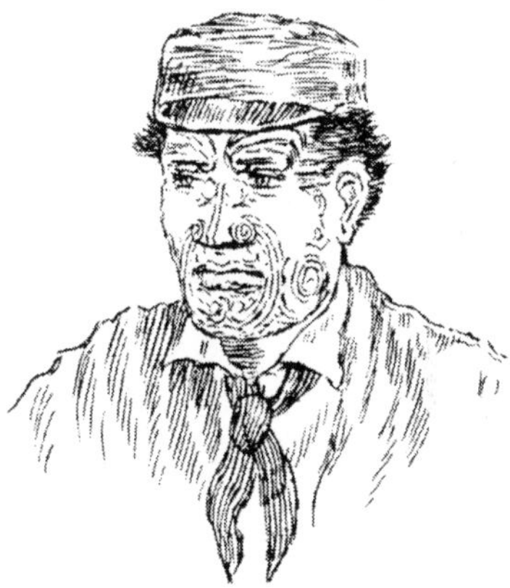

FIG. 129.—The engineer of the Gate Pa.
(*From a sketch from life by the Author, 1864.*)

when among the natives. There was difficulty in seeing much body-tattooing, as clothes were worn invariably. There are not many correct illustrations of it extant, nor many specimen skins in the museums, which illustrate the facial patterns plentifully. I give a list of some museums possessing good examples of moko at pp. 197—205.

I have, however, traced off one good thigh pattern, and give some portraits, copies, and photographs—one a war dance, another a fallen warrior in the fern. The effigies in wood show a quantity of good limb and body tattooing. Our last native visitors to England were a small contingent, including a girl amongst them, brought over by the Salvation Army in 1894. They were paraded in London. I sought them out in the hope of sketching a mokoed New Zealander once more from life; but in vain. The "major" of the party informed me that only girls here and there kept up tattooing and that the men had done with it. Then I realised that moko was done for and that the art vanishes. Would it be semi-barbarous to say

"Heu *moko* præteritos si referat Jupiter annos"?

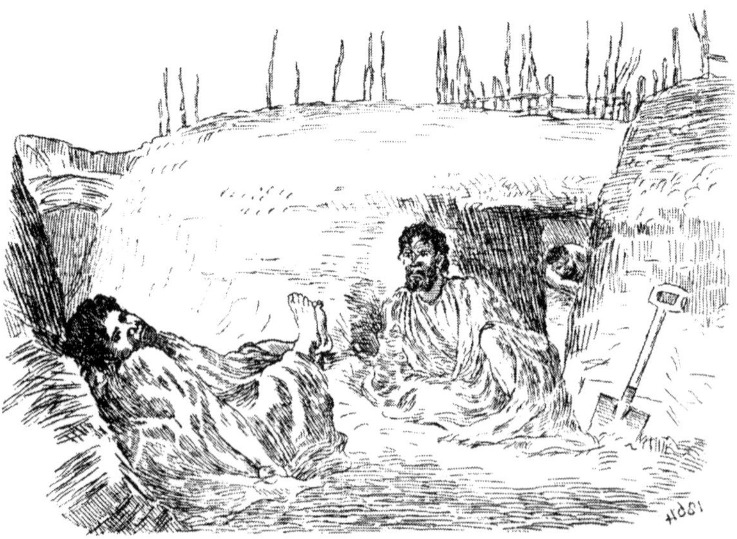

FIG. 130.—Wounded Maoris (with slight tattooing).
(*Sketch in the Rifle Pits 1864, by the Author.*)

PART II

MOKOMOKAI

Mokomokai was the name given to a dried head. The reverence paid it, whether it had belonged to a relative, a friend, or a foe, will be made apparent in these chapters. In this second part of the book I deal with the mokomokai, traditions and history, the method of embalming, and artists engaged. Next is shown the effects of the sudden demand for cured heads in exchange for trade purposes, the evils of this traffic, and its suppression; and, finally, some account of the best preserved heads in museums and private collections, distinguishing those specimens which show *post-mortem* moko. My object throughout is, however, to illustrate the art of moko and its interest as design.

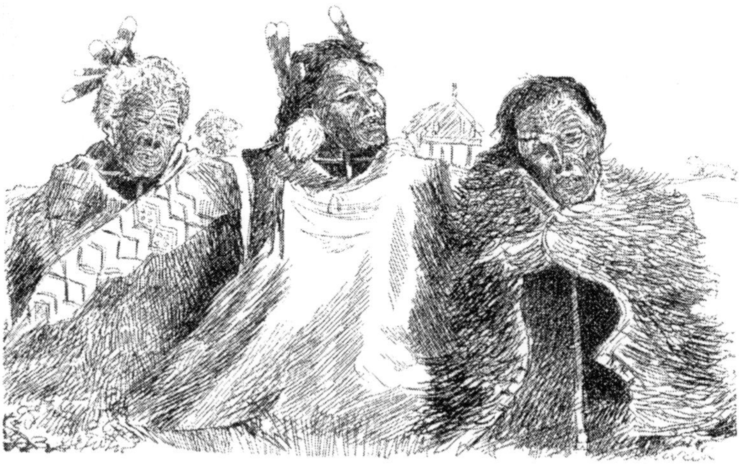

Fig. 131.—Preserved heads of Maori warriors arrayed in robes and displayed by their conquerors.

(From a sketch by the Author.)

CHAPTER X

TRADITION, HISTORY, AND INCIDENTS OF MOKOMOKAI

The curing or embalming of the head was among the Maoris an acknowledgment of the nobility of its owner: it served to keep alive the memory of the departed, among a people who were innocent of literature or of any (except carving) of the usual forms of art. Most of the early writers on New Zealand mention the practice of preserving human heads, and it appears to have been very general amongst the Maoris in their then state. None of the numerous accounts however are very complete, and many of them appear to be rather descriptions at second hand than records of personal observation. Probably this was due not so much to a lack of curiosity on the part of the writers as to the fact that observers were few, and would from prudential motives naturally keep aloof from the scenes of which the heads formed the central point of interest; besides which, in many cases, the actual business of preparation was strictly *tapu* or sacred, and an effectual bar would be placed against too minute a scrutiny. It is a question not only curious in itself, but of great interest to the ethnologist. Though the custom from a civilised point of view was certainly a barbarous one, it was not practised from mere brutality, or simply from a desire for personal vanity on the part of the conqueror; no dishonour was intended for the owner of the head, in fact the exact opposite was the case. The distinction, for such it was, was strictly reserved for persons of importance, and the heads of the chiefs of a tribe, and occasionally those of their wives and children, were preserved as well as these of the chiefs of the enemy slain in battle. Mr. Marsden states that "it is gratifying to the vanquished to know that the heads of their chiefs are preserved by the enemy"; and the same authority relates the case of a chief's wife who had the head of her sister preserved, and placed in an ark near her hut in order that she might relieve her feelings by weeping over it.

Moko being in old days an essential part of warlike preparations, it is more than probable that many a young brave was supported under the pain of tattooing by the thought of the handsome and warlike appearance it would give to his countenance whenever his head came to be preserved.

The principal object of the custom seems to have been to

keep alive the memory of the dead, and the mokomokai, as they were called, supplied the place of statues and pictures and

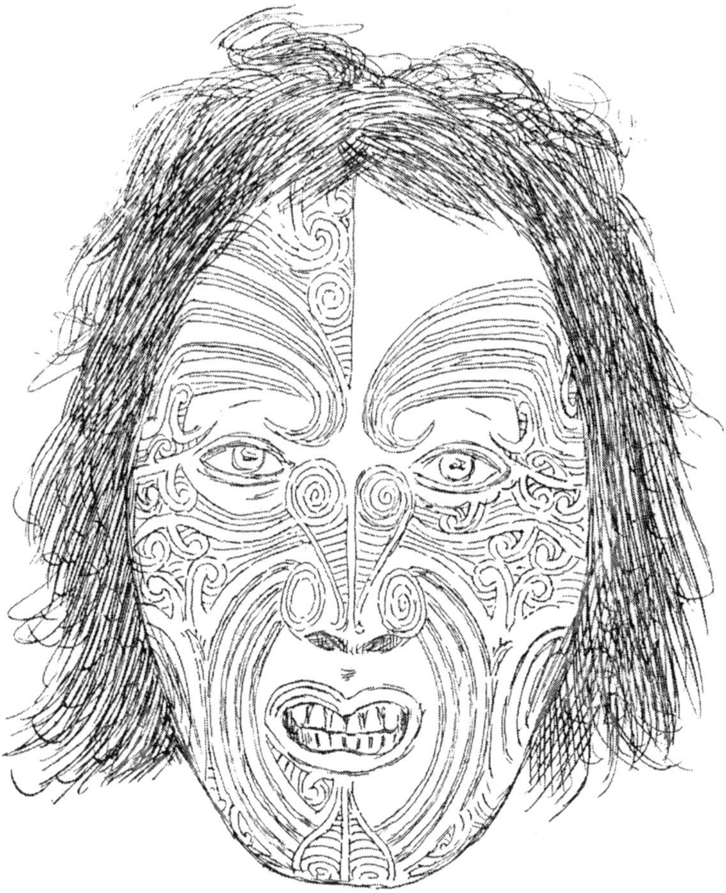

FIG. 132.—Specimen at Saffron Walden Museum: head of woman, with *post-mortem* tattooing only, probably done for sale.

monumental records. In the case of a departed chief of a tribe it was a visible sign that in some mysterious way his presence still dwelt amongst his people, inciting them to emulate his virtues, and to follow in his steps; while in that of the slaughtered warrior mokomokai served to keep alive the memory of the injury received by the tribe in whose possession they remained, and afforded a constant challenge to revenge and retaliation. Even where the mokoed head was that of an enemy, its possession was valued by the victorious tribe, and was only given up under circumstances of a peculiar nature. The preserved head of a foe was a familiar object about the old Maori *pas* and in its vicinity. The Rev. G. Smales says the enemies' heads were usually placed on the tops of houses or on poles by the wayside where they were exposed to the contemptuous taunts of the passers-by. Those of relations and friends were, however, more carefully kept. They were placed in a secluded spot; they were protected by the strictest *tapu;* they were brought forth and exhibited only on great occasions, as the *hahunga* (a feast attending the ceremonial raising of a chief's bones), at the departure of a warlike expedition, or at a gathering of the tribe.

During the progress of a war or when negotiations for peace were pending, these embalmed heads of the principal chiefs played no small part in the business of the moment. Mr. Marsden was informed by Hongi and Te Morenga that when a chief fell in combat the victors demanded that the body, if not already in their possession, should be delivered up, and this was done if his people considered further fighting to be useless. Hostilities were suspended, the head was cut off, and after an elaborate ceremony of "auguration" the *tohunga* (or priest) proclaimed the cessation or continuance of the fight. The head was kept for the chief on whose account war had been begun; it was preserved and sent round to relatives and friends as evidence that justice had been satisfied, and the war brought to an honourable conclusion.

Such are some of the earliest incidents we know attaching to mokomokai. The origin of embalming is involved in obscurity, in common with everything relating to the early customs of the people. No one knows whether the Maori brought the art with him, or evolved it from his consciousness or observation. It was in vogue before Cook came into the country. Mr. Yates says the custom of preserving enemies' heads was one of more recent date; and was an extension of the older custom of preserving the heads of friends and relatives. As a matter of fact, when the traffic (about which more anon) in heads became general, the Maoris ceased to preserve the heads of friends lest their relics should be sold. This traffic in dried heads will be told separately and presently.

Weight must be given to the consideration that warriors would wish to show as trophies the heads of the chiefs they had killed in combat. However, the evidence that this custom, as relating to enemies, was of more recent origin is satisfactory; and we must look to the older and pleasanter aspect of mokomokai—namely, the embalming of the heads of friends, as supplying the origin of the custom. Some confirmation of this view may be derived from the undoubtedly old custom of embalming the head of a beloved wife or child. And I shall proceed to deal with the two branches of the subject separately. But first I shall have to refer to the ethnological aspect of the matter in the shortest possible terms. The embalming of the Maori head does not only suggest the Egyptian mummy process. In Book IV. of his *History*, Herodotus tells us the Scythian warrior used to carry away the heads of his slain foes for preservation. It has been said the Gauls used to bring home and embalm the heads of defeated enemies, and that collections of these trophies were kept in large chests. The conserving of scalps by American Indians and even by the Scythians need hardly be referred to.

Mokomokai of Enemies.

Reference has been made to the custom of exposing an enemy's head, as contrasting with that of carefully guarding the head of a friend or relative. It should be added that Mr. White states these strange heads were set on the tops of the posts surrounding the marae or enclosure (courtyard, it may be rendered) so that strangers might see the results of the prowess of the tribe. They were a sort of *spolia opima* to the successful chief, over which he is supposed to exult. I give an illustration of three heads treated in the manner characteristic of the country; and about these the victors would relate to an admiring audience the tales of war and victory, and slay the slain again. At the conclusion of war, an exchange of heads was an indispensable article in the treaty of peace. Should a chief dispose of a captured head during the continuance of the war, it was regarded as a sign that he would never conclude peace with his foe. The exposed head was placed on a pole or stake (*turu turu*) with crossbars to represent arms; a mat was wrapped round pole and crossbar to give the effigy as life-like an appearance as circumstances would admit. On the occasion of a gathering of the clan or tribe, the victorious chief would gloat over these precious things, and re-enact the incidents of the combat amidst a scene of wild excitement. Mr. J. S. Polack says that in the flight of an army or in the butchery of prisoners, those heads that were best punctured were decollated for future preservation; but that the possessor of an unmarked head was battered and crushed with the most savage brutality. Subsequently those that were worth preserving, when set up on stakes as already described, were subject to all manners of abuse and obloquy from the victors who addressed the captured heads as though they were living persons. Mr. Yates thus renders the language addressed to these effigies of deceased enemies: "You wanted to run away, did you? But my *mere* overtook you, and after you were cooked you were made food for my mouth. And where is your father? He is cooked. Where is your brother? He is eaten. Where is your wife? There she sits, a wife for me. Where are your children? There they are, with loads on their backs, carrying food as my slaves."

Mr. T. B. Lee, native teacher of Waima, Hokianga, informed the Rev. P. Walsh, on the authority of a chief of that district, that the head of an obnoxious party would be dried, and, as an *ito,* would accompany its rangatira on fishing excursions, when it would be so fixed on the gunwale of the canoe as to nod freely if a fish took the baited hook, the line of which was attached to the ear.

Some hair was usually torn from the head of each slain enemy, and preserved for the home-coming of the victors.

So long as the heads remained in the possession of a victorious chief, no amicable relations were possible between the rival tribes. Sometimes where both sides were inclined for peace, it happened that the heads of defunct friends were exchanged, or purchased, and returned to the surviving relatives by whom they were held in much veneration. The number of these preserved heads must have been very considerable, and a parade or exhibition of them must have been a very terrible spectacle to a stranger. Mr. Marsden tells us that on the return of one of Hongi's expeditions against the East Coast natives, a single canoe brought back to Rangihou no less than seventy of these trophies. The early missionaries used to find, during the fighting season which lasted for several months, that the palisading of the adjacent Pa and even the fence of their own compounds were decorated with a row of heads. As before remarked, only the heads of chiefs or of the tattooed were thus preserved; and when the heads were those of enemies, restoration to the defeated tribe was an indispensable preliminary to peace. The most important part which they played, however, was during the actual progress of the war, and in the negotiations respecting its continuance or otherwise. These heads were consequently too precious to be traded away for the white man's treasures. A change was brought about in these views when Hongi first obtained a good supply of arms and ammunition. Hongi was the first to organise Maori warfare on this new principle, and the terror of his name spread far. Every effort was made to meet him on equal terms; but difficulty was experienced in buying enough arms and ammunition. A ton of dressed flax, laboriously scraped with a *pipi* shell, could only be bartered for a single gun. But when it was found that the trading schooner would give guns and ammunition for specimen heads, another state of things supervened. Mokoed heads were wanted, and were rapidly provided, for the drying process was such that new and old heads were not readily distinguished. And what was once an honour reserved for chiefs, became forced on slaves with a view to prompt sale of the head. So armaments were bought; and the traders got that which the public wanted for museums and for collections. Then came the end, as we shall see.

It will have been gathered from what has been said that the Maoris did not entirely reserve their treatment of heads solely for their own race; and many heads of white men have been similarly smoked and dried. An instance may be given: In 1834, H.M.S. *Alligator* was sent to obtain restoration of British subjects, then in the hands of the New Zealanders; after the affair at Waimati on the coast, the preserved head of some ill-fated European was taken out of the water which partially filled a trench, where it was supposed to have been thrown on the flight of the natives. The complexion of this head was changed, but the features and hair remained unaltered. This discovery formed a melancholy confirmation of Mr. Guard's tale of shipwreck and slaughter. Yet, strange to say, none of the survivors of the crew of the *Harriet* could recognise the face as one of their former companions, and it may have been obtained from another source. The sight of the head again stirred up the soldiers, and in the course of the day one of them brought in the head of a New Zealander which he had detached from the trunk of one of the fallen natives. It was, however, buried by the officers under a rock, as it had been made a football of. The last instance is from the fighting which occurred in 1864. Just when the Maori cause seemed lost, the flames of war were fanned by a new religion called the *Pai Marire* or *Hauhau*, derived from the "fightingest" part of the Bible. At Te Ahuhu, on April 6th, a detachment under Captain P. W. J. Lloyd, of the 57th Regiment, was cut off in an ambuscade. Captain Lloyd fell fighting heroically, and killed or wounded three natives with his revolver when lying on the ground with a broken thigh. His body had eighteen wounds. The natives, believing that a British medical officer had decapitated one of their people and carried off his head as a specimen, did it for *Utu*, or revenge. They cut off the heads of Captain Lloyd and the fallen of his party, and having drunk their blood, they buried the heads and bodies in separate places. A few days after, they dug up the heads and smoked and dried them in the old fashion. Captain Lloyd's head was placed on a pole at Pipiriki on the Wanganui river and subjected to indignity; the wild fanatics even rushing at it and *biting* at it. The Hauhaus believed that the Angel Gabriel would appear to those who drank of the blood; and they caused the head to be carried about in order that it might be a means of communicating with Jehovah. They then announced that the head had appointed a high-priest *Te Ua* and two assistant prophets, *Hepania* and *Rangitauria;* had communicated a new religion; and that its believers (called Very Good) were to be protected by the Angel Gabriel and his legions who would aid in driving the Europeans out of the country, together with all natives who did not adopt the new faith. When this was accomplished, messengers would come from heaven and teach the Maoris all the *Pakeha* arts and sciences. A head was afterwards given up at Waitotara by *Te Ua* to Mr. Brompton, the interpreter; and the officers of the 57th believed it to be that of their gallant comrade. It was buried with the body, and a lock of hair sent to the widow.

In March, 1865, during the continuance of the fanaticism, the Rev. Mr. Volckner was killed at Opitiki, and shocking orgies ensued. Later in the same year the head of a soldier was taken to Pipiriki by Kereopa and Patara, and used as a mystic symbol. This is the last case of an English head preserved in the Maori fashion. In 1827 Captain Dillon was ordered by the Government of British India to undertake a voyage to the South Seas to ascertain the fate of La Perouse's expedition. In the course of the voyage, he was informed that the ship's carpenter had refused to work, and said he was going ashore. To deter him from this step Captain Dillon had recourse to the following expedient. He asked him if he had seen any preserved human heads offered for sale by the natives since his arrival. The carpenter replied he had. "Then, sir," said Captain Dillon, "if you attempt to desert from the ship I will pay the natives to preserve your head and bring it here as a curiosity." The threat had the desired effect.

I have myself seen the mokomokai of a young European, with close cropped hair. How old it was I could not judge.

As already stated, these preserved heads of native enemies had their use in bringing about peace, and often in maintaining it when once arranged.

It may be added that after the Maori had knowledge of fire-arms, the skin of the buttocks of a dead enemy, if well tattooed, was stripped off; it is about one-fifth of an inch thick, and was used as a cover for cartouche-boxes. In a medical museum I can name, there is a bit or sample of tanned skin of a man (name given) which is equal to good quality pig skin. On the same shelf is a small white-looking taper or uncanny dip formed of human fat. Commerce, one may suppose, will not adopt these articles just yet. (One reads lately that in France after the execution of the murderer Pranzini, the presiding judge was presented with a purse made from the criminal's skin.) I will endeavour to exhaust all I have to tell of these old Maori practices with a short account given by Captain Cruise, when at the Bay of Islands. The English learnt one day on going ashore that a body of natives had just returned from a successful expedition with numerous prisoners, including men, women, and children, some of the latter not two years old. Amongst the prisoners was one distinguished by her superior beauty, who sat apart from the rest on the beach, and though silent seemed buried in affliction. Her father, it appeared, had been killed by the man whose prisoner she had become, and who remained near her during the greater part of the day. The gruesome narrative proceeds:

"As we were preparing to return to the ship, we were drawn to that part of the beach where the prisoners were by the most doleful cries and lamentations. Here was the interesting young slave in a situation that ought to have softened the heart of the most unfeeling. The man who had slain her father, having cut off his head and preserved it by a process peculiar to these islanders, took it out of a basket, and threw it into the lap of the unhappy daughter. At once she seized it with a degree of frenzy not to be described; and subsequently with a bit of sharp shell disfigured her person in so shocking a manner that in a few minutes not a vestige of her former beauty remained."

They afterwards learnt that this fellow had married the very woman whom he had treated with such singular barbarity.

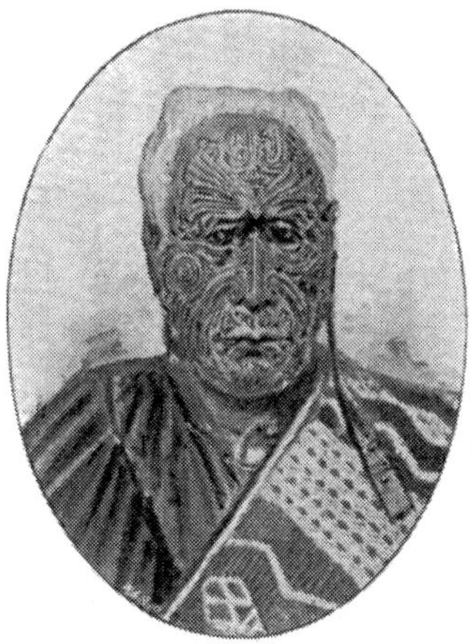

Fig. 133.—Taraia: (a chief who cooked two native Christians in 1842,) fully tattooed, fine specimen.

I will record the last act of cannibalism which is associated, as so many are, with heads. This ancient Maori custom was used for the last time at Katikati on the Thames about fifty miles from Auckland; and two human beings were cooked and eaten in 1842. They were native Christians. They fell in an attack led by a chief called Taraia, who had a feud against them, and they were duly entombed in the stomachs of the victors. The native account of the affair was reported to the New Zealand Government, as follows: After the action Taraia reached his own village where there were a church and a few believers, and here they rang the prayer-bell. When the Christian natives were at evening worship, Taraia rolled the two heads out into the midst of them. The missionaries were sent for by the executive council, and they proposed to Taraia that he should give some compensation to the sufferers' tribe. To this Taraia made no objection provided that the tribe in question paid him for the relations they had slain. "Have they not eaten my mother?" said Taraia. The matter was allowed to rest there; but it is satisfactory to give the portrait of the so-called last of the Cannibals.

Mokomokai of Friends.

The heads of their relatives were always objects of the greatest esteem to the Maoris; and here we touch upon pleasanter subjects. Families kept their relics in boxes, and aired them on occasion with songs and praises. Dieffenbach says: "In the vestibule of one of the houses I found the head of a young girl in a basket prepared in the manner which has long been so well known, and of which so many examples have been conveyed to Europe." They were preserved as a memorial of the grief of survivors, or to show to relatives who might have been absent at the decease. It may be compared to the operations on the deceased performed by the ancient Egyptian physician and priest. Some light is thrown on the matter by a narration in Mr. Earle's book. Speaking of the return of a warlike expedition in 1837, he says: "They had brought with them several heads which they have the art of pre paring in their native ovens, so as not to disfigure the countenance nor injure the figure tattooed upon them. One of these, the skull of a distinguished chief, seemed to afford them amazing delight. Most of our people had known him well, and several of his near

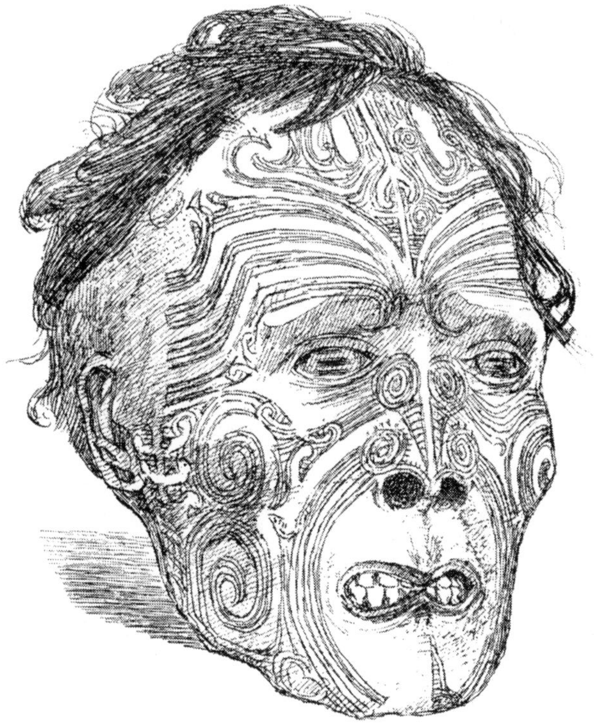

FIG. 134.—A specimen in Author's collection—head preserved by friend showing var; pattern on cheeks.

relatives were present; but cruel war seemed to have eradicated every feeling of humanity, for all appeared to contemplate this ghastly object with great satisfaction. These heads were decorated profusely with yellow and red ribbons, and with white feathers;

they were then stuck upon short poles and placed with great ceremony in front of old Queen Turero's house, who, sitting at the door, received this token of respect with approval and condescension."

This passage also hints at the method which was adopted to embalm the head. If the deceased had relatives, the operators removed to some distance from their habitation; and neither

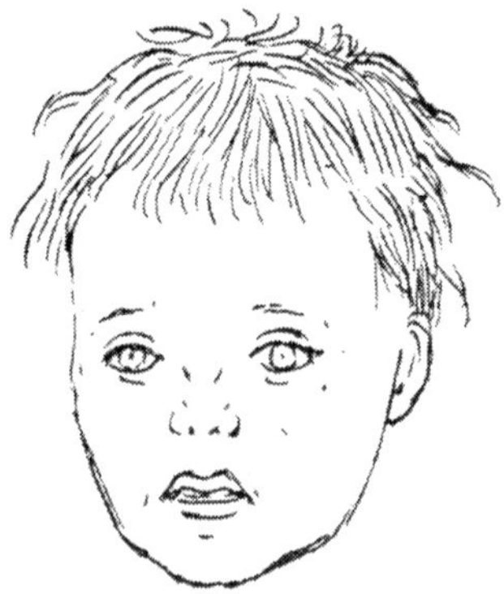

FIG. 135.—Preserved head of a Maori baby (in King's College Museum, London), with gray glass eyes added by a European taxidermist.

operators nor relatives were allowed to touch food until the head was fully "cured." All were *tapu;* for if the process were witnessed by the friends, they would, we are told, be unable to repress their tears, and the head would be spoilt. The reasoning seems to lack something, but in the case of an enemy's head the operation was publicly performed. My illustrations will show the careful observer a case where the lips of the embalmed head are sewn together. This will explain another important distinction between a friend's head and that of an enemy. In the case of an enemy the lips are stretched out and sewn apart, while in the case of a friend the lips were sewn close together as though pouting. The Rev. Mr. Taylor says that it was no uncommon thing to embalm in this way the head of a favourite wife or child. The heads of these and of other relatives were preserved in baskets carefully made and scented with oil. They were brought out to be honourably mourned over, and on these occasions they were decorated with feathers and placed in a conspicuous position. In former times the principal wife of a deceased chief would have her husband's head cut off and dried, and also sleep with it by her side.

CHAPTER XI

METHODS OF EMBALMING

We are fortunate enough in recording the history of moko to have fairly full accounts of the process of mokomokai. The Rev. Mr. Taylor says the preparation of the skull was called *Paki Paki*, or *Popo*, which signified taking out the brain. The heads were then steamed in the oven several times, and after each steaming were carefully wiped with the flowers of the *kakaho* or reed, and every portion of flesh and brain was removed, a small thin *manuka* stick being inserted between the skin and bone of the nose to preserve its form. This over, the heads were dried in the sun, and afterwards exposed to the smoke of their houses. The eyes were extracted, the sockets filled with flax, and the lids sewn together. The heads thus prepared were exempt from the attacks of insects, being thoroughly impregnated with pyroligneous acid. At the neck, where the head had been severed from the body, the skin was drawn together like the mouth of a bladder tobacco-pouch, leaving an open space large enough to admit the hand, as a portion of the base of the skull was cut away.

The Rev. Philip Walsh, in an interesting paper read before the Auckland Institute, in October, 1894, says: "Those seen by

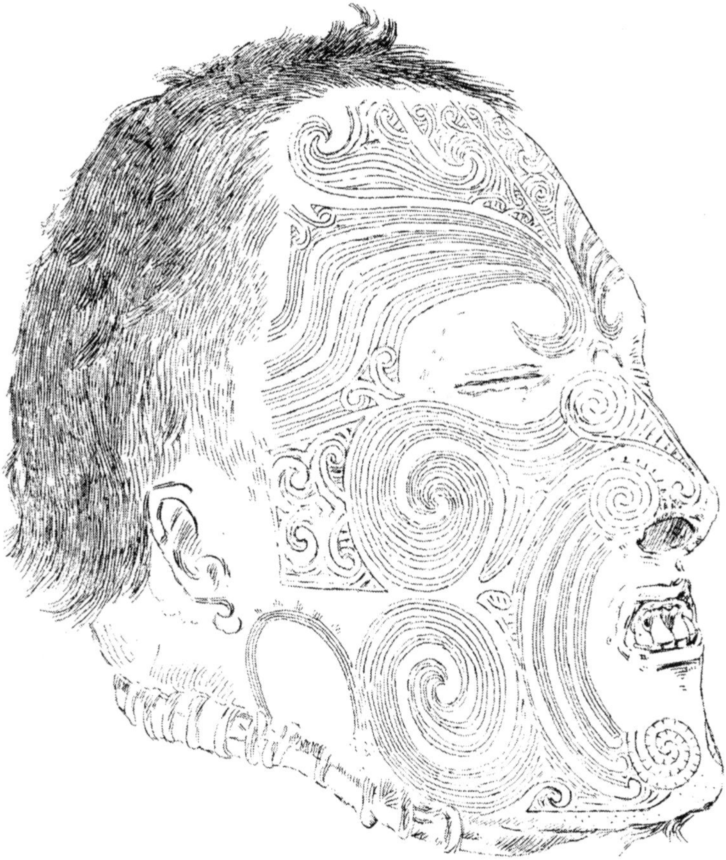

Fig. 136.—Specimen in Author's collection.

Mr. King were impaled on upright sticks set in open holes in the ground, which were kept supplied with hot stones from a fire close by, while the operator basted them with melted fat. Each of these processes would equally serve the purpose required. The

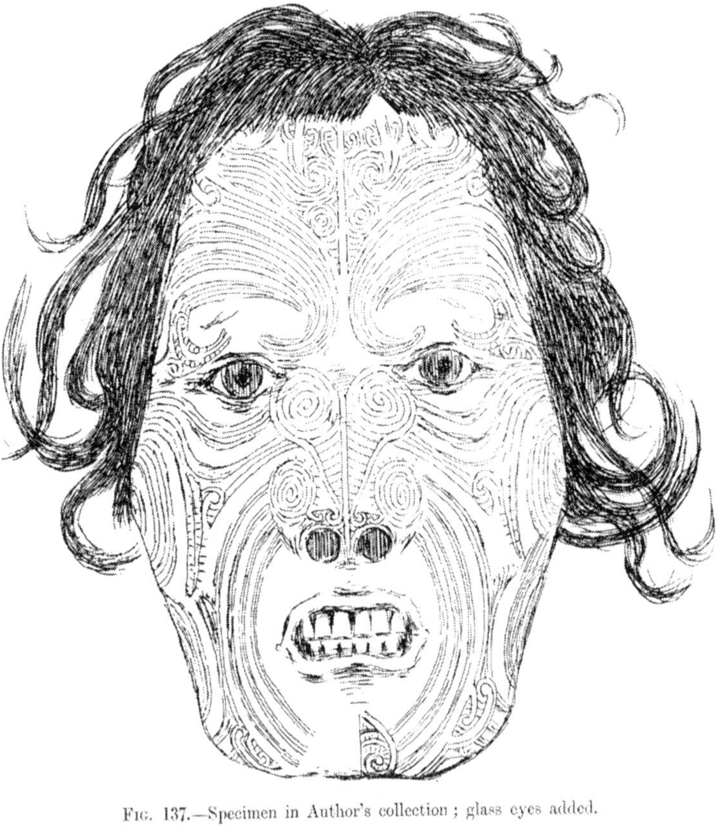

Fig. 137.—Specimen in Author's collection; glass eyes added.

next stage was a thorough desiccation effected by an alternate exposure to the rays of the sun and the fumes of a wood fire, of which the pyroligneous acid helped to preserve the tissues and protect them from the ravages of insects. A finishing touch was given by anointing the head with oil and combing back the hair into a knob on the top, which was ornamented with feathers, those of the albatross being usually preferred. The work was then complete. The form of the features was very fairly preserved; every line of the moko was distinct; although the likeness was sufficient to identify the departed warrior, the heads invariably bore a

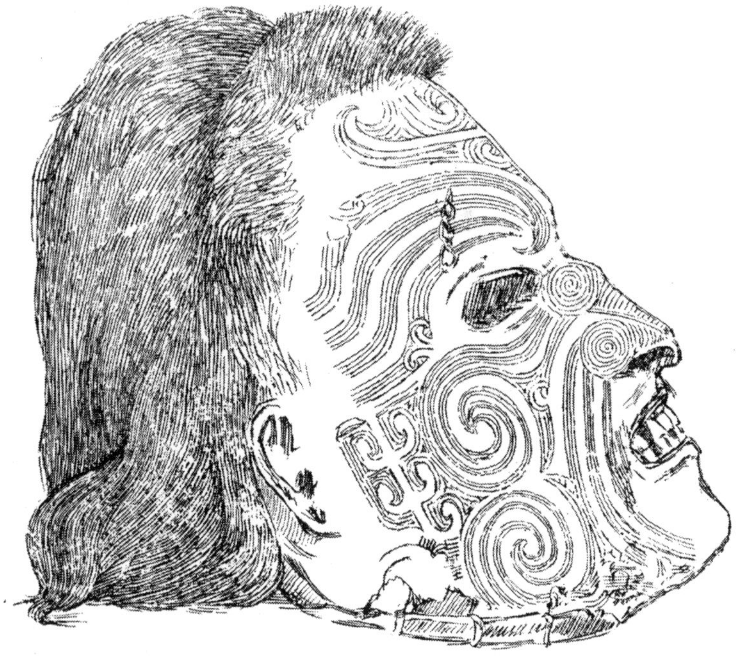

FIG. 138.—Specimen in Author's collection; lips with blue dye.

ghastly expression of life-in-death which once seen can never be forgotten.

Captain Cruise's account corroborates this; but the most

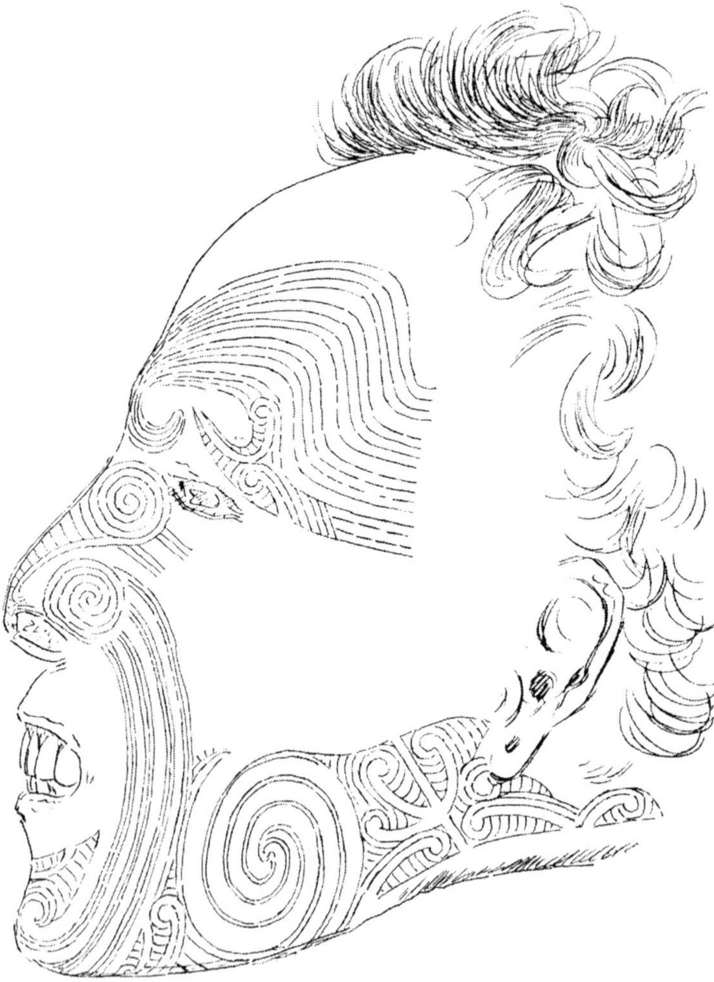

Fig. 139.—Specimen in Author's collection showing tattooing on neck.

interesting is that of Rutherford, whom the reader will remember as the shipwrecked sailor who became a Maori chief. He is on the

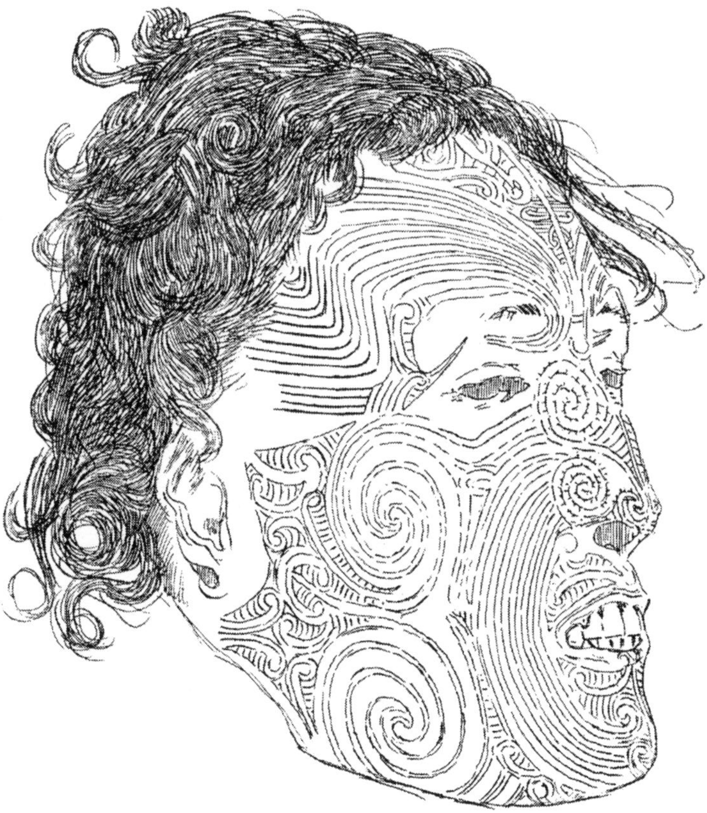

FIG. 140.—Specimen in Author's collection, fully tattooed head.

subject of mokomokai as minute and detailed in his remarks as he is on most points he touches; and his accuracy is not, I think, to be questioned. According to him, the skull was first completely emptied, the eyes and tongue extracted, after which the nostrils and whole interior of the head were stuffed with flax.

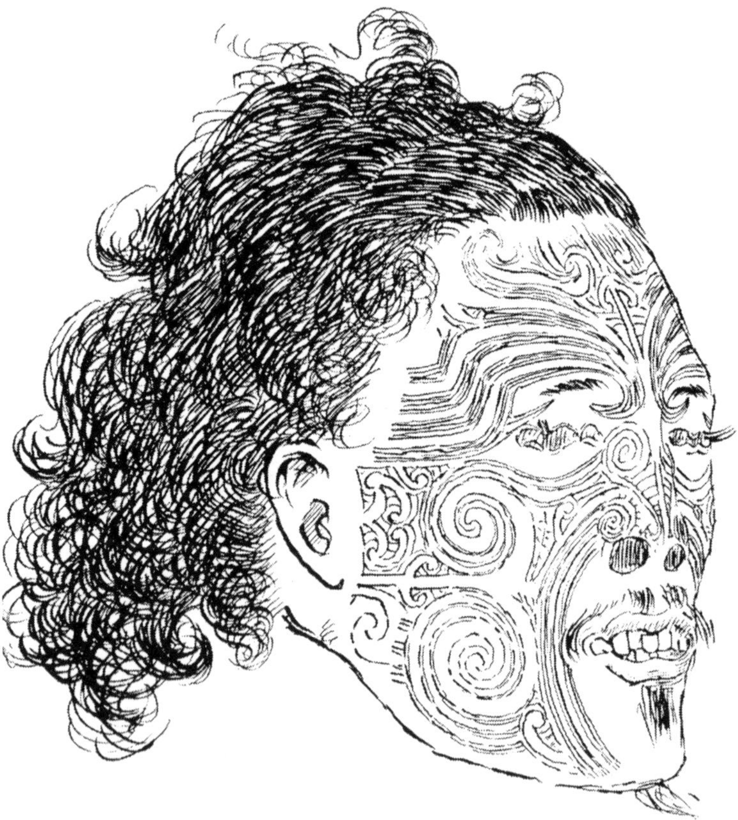

FIG. 141—Specimen in Author's collection, showing work done with fine instruments.

The head was then wrapped up in a quantity of green leaves, and in this state exposed to the fire till well steamed. The leaves were then removed, and it was hung up to dry in smoke, causing the flesh to become tough and hard. The hair and teeth were preserved, and the face-moko was seen as well as in a living person. The head thus cured would, if not exposed to damp, long maintain its appearance. I may remark that Captain Cruise speaks only of a current of dry air and not of smoke as being the drying medium; but I think a large part of the preservative element was due to smoke of a wood fire. It is very probable that the

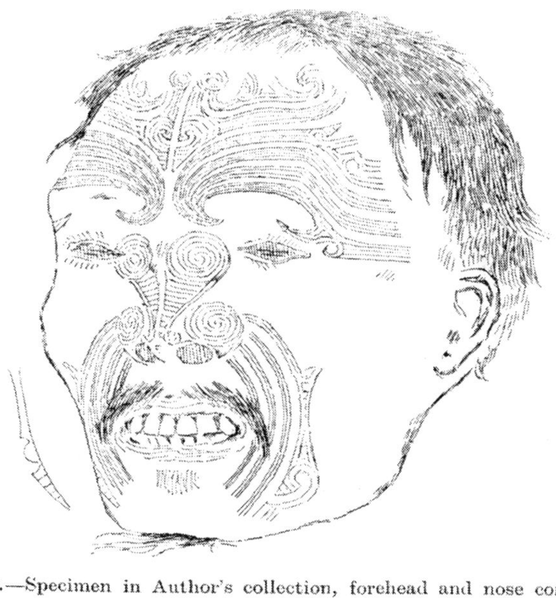

FIG. 142.—Specimen in Author's collection, forehead and nose completed.

various artists purposely differed in their methods of treatment in their efforts to acquire an enviable distinction, and it is not unlikely that in the case of the more distinguished subjects extra care would be taken, and a more elaborate system employed.

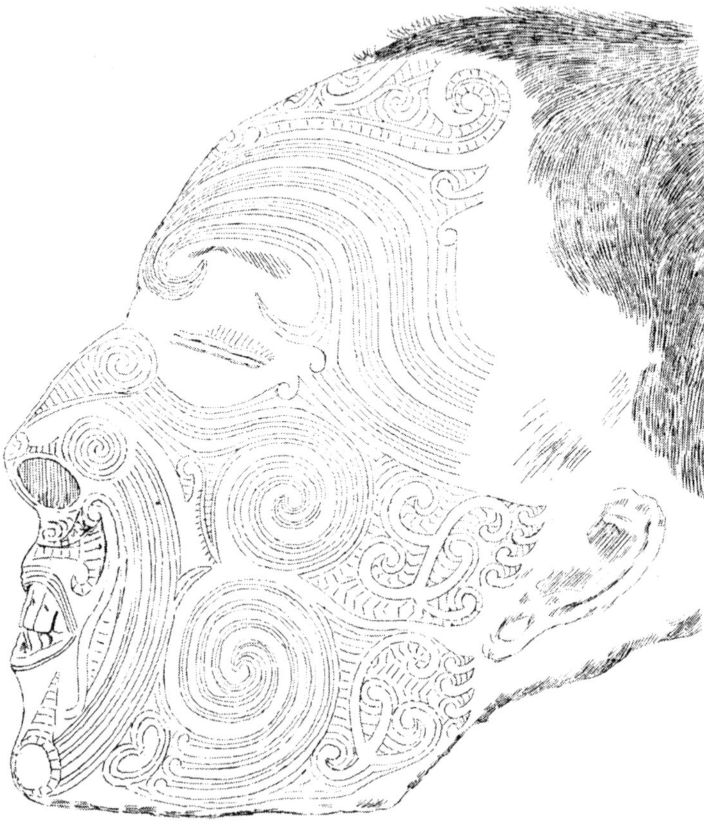

Fig. 143.—Specimen in Author's collection.

It may be here noted that a French writer regards the Maori art of preserving heads as showing original connection between the New Zealanders and the ancient world; and he compares their processes with that of the Egyptians in embalming mummies. This question, however, extends far beyond the limits of ascertainable fact.

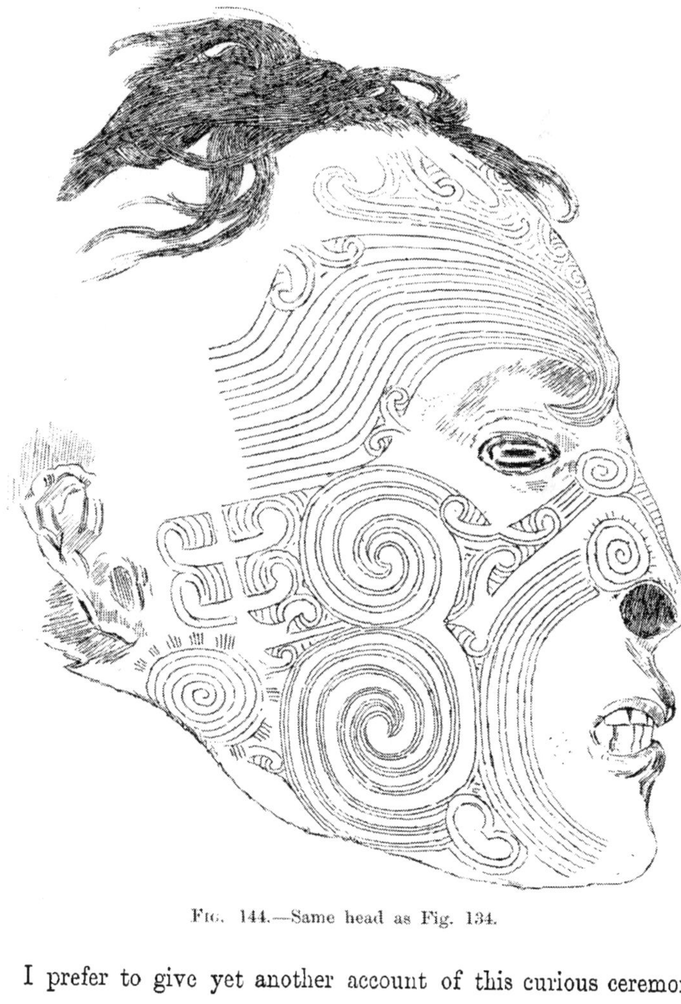

FIG. 144.—Same head as Fig. 134.

I prefer to give yet another account of this curious ceremony from the Rev. William Yates, who as a missionary of the Church

Missionary Society in the North Island in 1835, had no small experience of Maori life before its change established itself. He says: "The following account of the process was given me by a chief who has preserved and assisted in preserving many after the various battles in which he had engaged. When the head has been cut off the shoulders, the brains are immediately taken out through a perforation behind, and the skull carefully cleaned inside from all mucilaginous and fleshy matter. The eyes are then scooped out, and the head thrown into boiling water, into which red-hot stones are continually cast to keep up the heat. It remains till the skin will slip off, and is then suddenly plunged into cold water, whence it is immediately taken and placed in a native oven, so as to allow the steam to penetrate into all the cavities of the interior of the skull. When sufficiently steamed, it is placed on a stick to dry, and again put into an oven made for the purpose, about the size of the head. The flesh, which easily slips off the bones, is then taken away, and small sticks are employed to thrust flax or the bark of trees within the skin so as to restore it to its former shape and preserve the features. The nostrils are carefully stuffed with a piece of fern root, and the lips generally sewn together; though sometimes they are not closed, but the teeth are allowed to appear. It is finished by hanging it for a few days to dry in the sun. Should the head not now be perfectly preserved, which is but rarely the case, or should there be any internal or external appearance of putrefaction, it is again steamed. This operation is continued till the skin is thoroughly dry, and all other soft matter removed or destroyed, so as to insure it against decomposition, unless much exposed to a humid atmosphere."

A good deal of the bones of the palate, nose, and interior, is sometimes cut away, and more or less flax used for stuffing the nose and cheeks. The great beauty of the Maori, namely his teeth, is well seen. It may be mentioned here that the expression "Upoko Kohue" or boiled head was the deepest insult known to the Maori language.

When the head of a friend is preserved, as is the case on his being slain in battle, and it has not been possible to carry off the

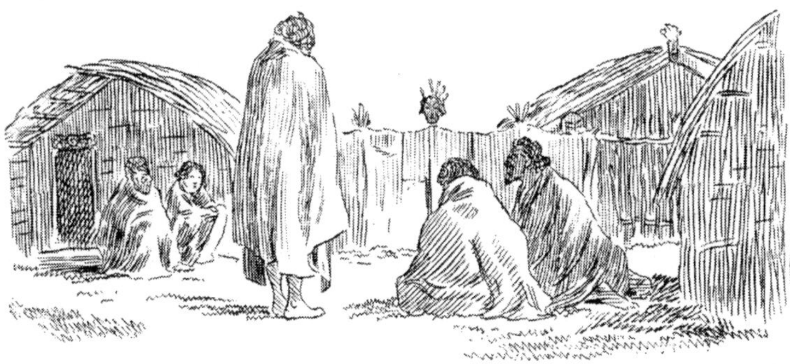

FIG. 145.—Mourning over the head of a friend.
(*After the Rev. Mr. Yates.*)

whole body, the head is deposited in the sacred grove; and when a friend or near relation visits the village, it is taken out in order that he may weep over it, and cherish the spirit of revenge against those by whom he fell. The head is generally placed in some conspicuous part of the residence on a piece of fence, or on the ornament of the roof over the doorway of a house. The stranger is then led to the spot, and his eyes are directed to the ghastly object before him; when he immediately assumes the attitude of grief. He stands in front of the skeleton head with his body bent almost to the earth, the big tear rolling down his manly cheeks, and in the most melancholy tones gives utterance to the over-powering feelings of his heart; till at length, as his grief subsides, he works himself into a fit of rage bordering on madness, at which time it is well for all poor slaves, both male and female, to keep out of sight, or he might slay one as a satisfaction to the trunkless head of his friend, which is placed before him. When the ceremony is concluded, the head is rolled again in its grave-clothes, and carefully deposited in the burial place till required again to excite the passions of some other friend.

I give a drawing of the enlarged opening at the base of the dried head, the aperture being wide enough to admit the hand. The rim of the aperture is generally bound with hoop and flax. The smoking of the head has different effects on its colour and appearance. Some heads are brown, some yellow, some even reddish. But all preserve the pattern of the moko. It is noticeable, too, that the eyelids in dried heads are usually closed, unless the natural eyes were kept or false ones added. The Maoris feared they would be bewitched if they looked into the empty sockets. The eyes were no doubt difficult to preserve even when left in the head. The Maori warrior had a way of gouging out the eyes of a vanquished chief and of swallowing them, thinking that he thus incorporated the dead man's spirit. The *Atua tonga* (divinity or soul) was thought to be located in the eyes—each eye was believed to have a separate immortality—the left eye ascending to heaven, and becoming a star, unless swallowed promptly, the right eye becoming a spirit and taking flight for the Reinga or leaping-place unless similarly "incorporated" by the victor. Latourneaux has carefully worked out these picturesque details for the instruction of modern writers. He adds that the greatest importance was attached to the eating of the left eye. In my drawing of a dried head at Saffron Walden, false eyes have been added to the head; and the earliest mention of dried heads in Captain Cook's writings refers to heads with false

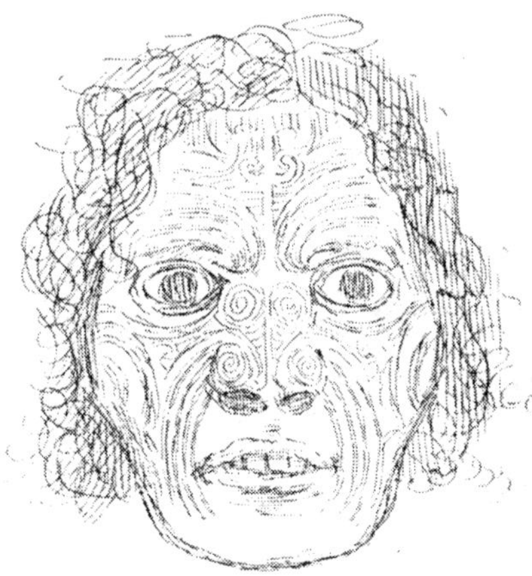

FIG. 146.—Head with false eyes inserted by native taxidermist. (*Saffron Walden Museum.*)

eyes. So the eyes of a chief slain in battle were generally missing; these scooped out and swallowed, his vanquisher obtained the spirit and power of the slain, and was raised above his fellows, becoming, if he swallowed enough, a god even upon earth and after death a heavenly luminary of the first magnitude. Of course attempts were made by the chief's friends in battle to preserve him from such a fate as loss of eyes. There is a fine specimen in my collection, where the original eyes have been well preserved. They are shrunk and look like raisins. I give a drawing, too, of a head in another collection, the head of a boy with *post-mortem* moko. The left eye is gone, but the right eye is well preserved. There is in a provincial museum the dried head of a woman with eyes well preserved; her moko is *post mortem*, and was possibly done by the

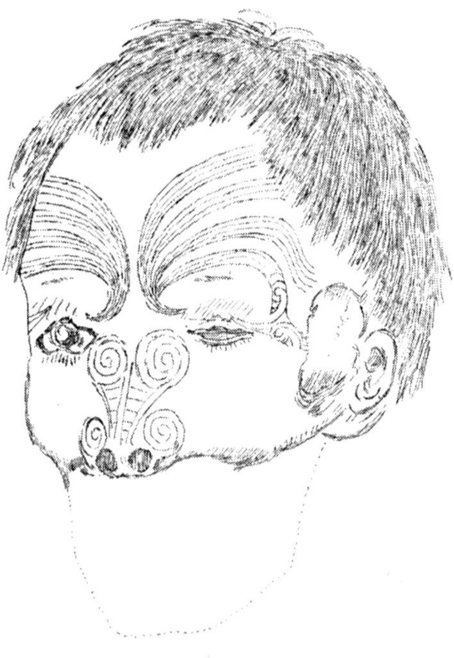

Fig. 147.—Head of a boy with *post-mortem* moko, in the possession of J. W. Colmer, Esq.

possessor of the head for purposes of sale (Fig. 132). The finishing touches were given to the embalmed head with oil, careful decoration of the hair with feathers, and equally careful combing and tying of the hair in a knot at the back of the head. In the result the features were preserved, and the identity of the deceased easily recognised.

I will quote here an extract from the *Fourth Annual Report of the Bureau of Ethnology* (1882–3) of the Smithsonian Institu-

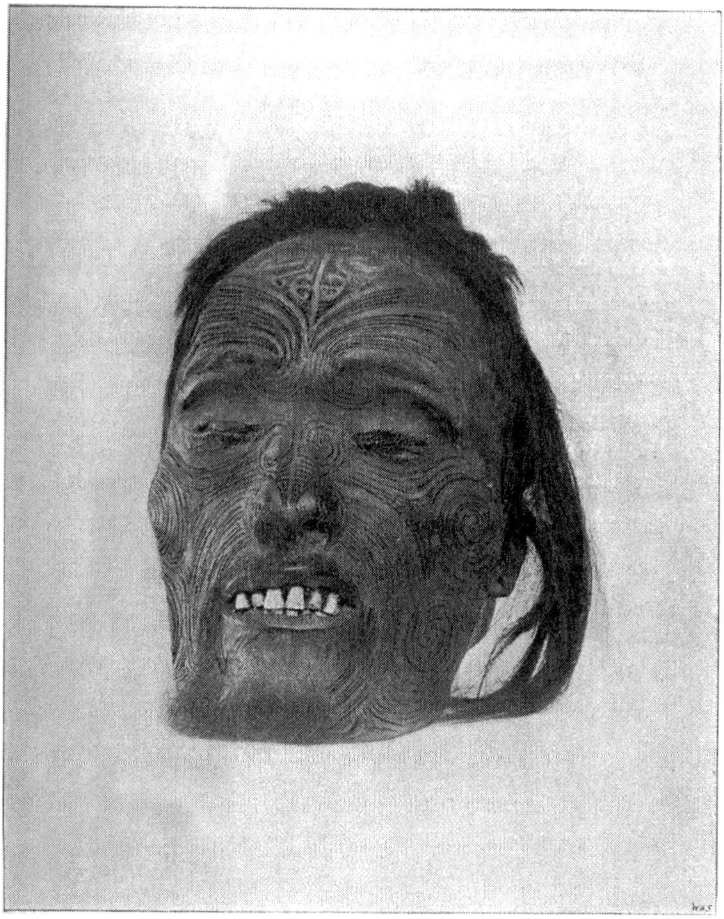

FIG. 148.—Specimen in Author's Collection.

tion, Washington, D.C., dated 1885 (p. 75): "Two beautifully tattooed heads are in the collection of the Army Medical Museum at Washington, D.C., of which illustrations are presented in the accompanying Plate III. No history of these heads can be obtained. The skin is almost perfect, and has become much brighter in tint than the original colour. The tattooing is a blue-black and in certain lights becomes almost bright indigo. In many of the markings there appear slight grooves, which add greatly to the general ornamentation, breaking the monotony of usually plain surfaces. Whether any mechanical work was performed upon the heads after death is not positively known, though from the general appearance of the work it would be suggested that the sharp creases or grooves were done subsequent to the death of the individual. The tattooing shows subcutaneous colouring, which indicates that at least part of the ornamentation was done in life."

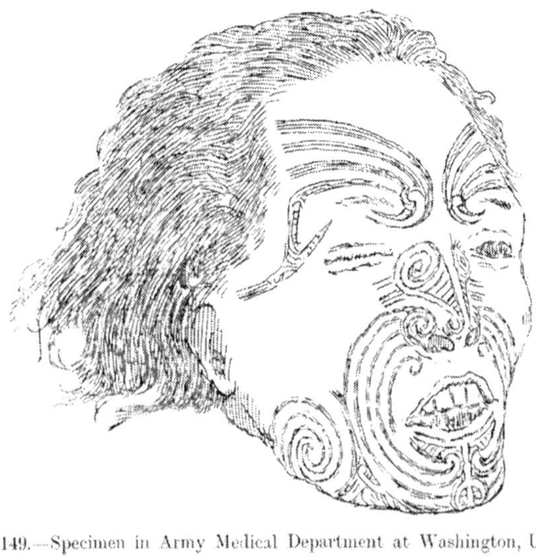

FIG. 149.—Specimen in Army Medical Department at Washington, U.S.A.

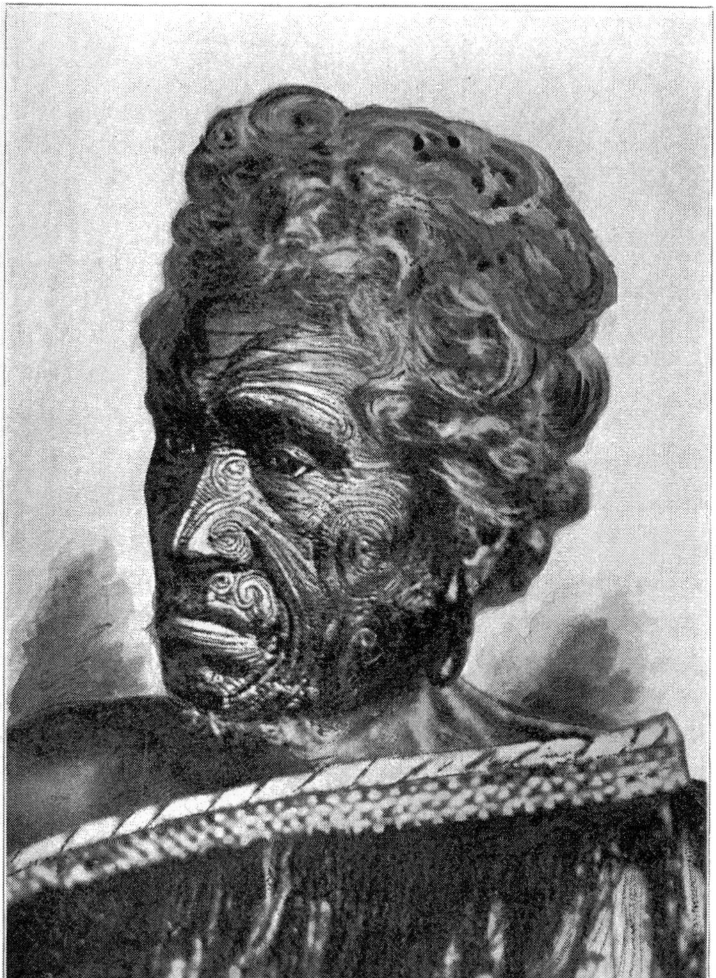

FIG. 150.—Head of a Chief.

CHAPTER XII

TRAFFIC IN HEADS

I WILL commence my remarks on the growth of the remarkable traffic in Maori dried heads with an account of a battle as given by Rutherford—an eye-witness—in his graphic narrative over seventy years ago. From such a battle as that which he speaks of, the traders derived no small advantage; and the traffic became so great a scandal that in 1831 it was stopped by legislation. Rutherford says: "The two bodies then advanced to within about one hundred yards of each other, when they fired their muskets. They only fired once, and then throwing their muskets behind them, where they were picked up by the women and boys, drew their meres or tomahawks out of their belts; when the war-song was being screamed by the whole of them together, in a manner most dismal to be heard, the two parties rushed into close combat. They now took hold of the hair of each others' heads with their left hands, using the right to cut off the head. Meanwhile, the women and boys followed close behind, uttering the most shocking cries I ever heard. These last received the heads of the slain from those engaged in the battle as soon as they were cut off, after which the men went in amongst the enemy for the dead bodies, but many of them received bodies that did not belong to the heads they had cut off."

The first dried head ever possessed by a European was acquired on January 20th, 1770. It was bought by Mr. (afterwards Sir Joseph) Banks, who was with Captain Cook's expedition as a naturalist; and it was one of four brought on board the *Endeavour* for inspection. It was the head of a youth of fourteen or fifteen, who had been killed by a blow that had fractured his skull. The three other heads, not for sale, seemed to have false eyes and ornaments in the ears. In Hawksworth's *Voyages of Captain Cook* it is recorded that the first head brought had been preserved, for it had no disagreeable smell, though from the softness of the skin it was evidently that of a person recently killed. The natives showed the greatest reluctance to sell the head, and could not be induced to part with another at that time. This reluctance, as we shall see, disappeared too soon. To get muskets wherewith to continue their terrible tribal wars, heads were soon sold, when it was found that a demand existed, and the demands of the traders were prompted by the prices paid by museums and collectors. Many a murderous attack, says Mr. Taylor, has been made to obtain heads for market, the best prices being paid for finely tattooed specimens. Mr. Taylor also says that he was assured some heads offered for sale were those of Europeans. Mr. Polack says that many a battle and predatory excursion has been undertaken expressly to obtain "choice tattooed heads" for white traders. Up to 1818 the native population was large. Fire-arms were extensively used after 1820, when heads became much cheaper, and European museums and collections well stocked. In my Appendix I have given a list of some of the collections. It was the desire to possess muskets for self-preservation, and the facility for exchanging dried heads for

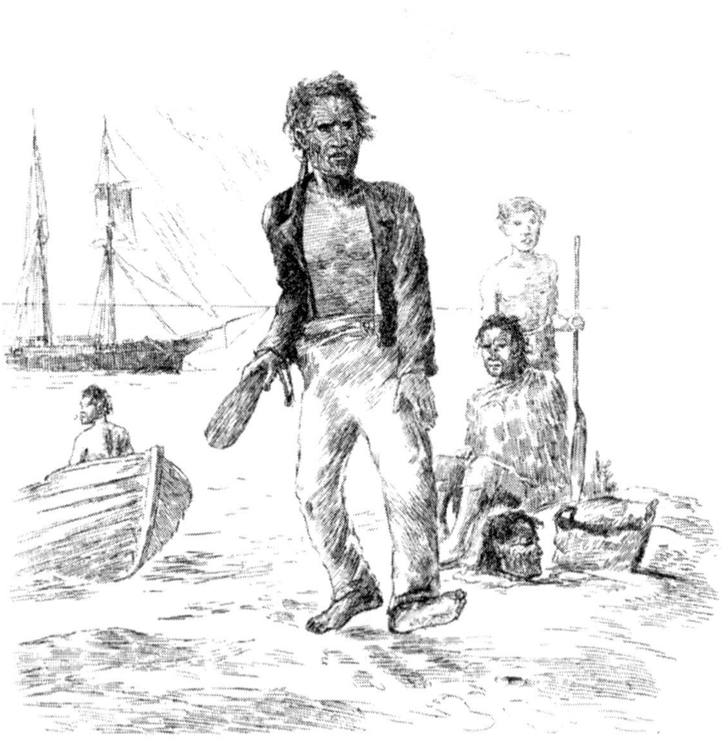

Fig. 151.—Bargaining for a head, on the shore, the chief running up the price. (*From a drawing by the Author.*)

firearms that led up to this traffic. There are instances of several white heads having been included in the trade in specimens. Between the years 1770–1809 only, upwards of one hundred Europeans had been killed and eaten in New Zealand.

The first head taken to Sydney, of which there is any record, was brought from Fouveaux Straits in 1811. It was obtained by theft, and a boat's crew was nearly cut off for *utu* (revenge). In 1814 heads were certainly not yet an ordinary article of trade at Sydney; but in 1820 it appears that preserved heads were not uncommon. Until Europeans began to visit New Zealand and to settle there, heads were of sentimental interest only and had no commercial value. But the desire to possess them as curiosities for museums and collectors, caused a large demand to spring up. The Maori on his part was eager to obtain firearms, ammunition, and iron implements. His reluctance to part with the heads was overcome, and so brisk a traffic sprang up that the demand exceeded the supply. It considerably reduced the population of New Zealand; but stocked the museums of Europe with specimens of barbaric face-culture; while as a commercial enterprise the traffic was not without profit. Freshly done and inferior heads took the place of the old and genuine; and it was found that a newly tattooed head looked as well when preserved as one similarly preserved years before. The chiefs were not slow in taking advantage of the discovery, and set to work to kill the least valuable of their slaves, tattooing their heads first (as above remarked) as though they had belonged to men of high rank, drying them and then selling them. The Rev. J. S. Wood says: "In the first place no man who was well tattooed was safe for an hour unless he was a great chief, for he might be at any time watched until he was off his guard and then knocked down and killed, and his head sold to the traders." Old grudges were raked up and small local wars undertaken to keep up the supply.

Many a poor slave suffered a horrible fate—mokoed only to be murdered for his head. At one time forbidden the pride of the noble and the free, the unhappy slave was now forcibly tattooed, and when his scars were healed he was tomahawked, his head dried, and then sold to the ever ready trader. A good-looking slave might be elaborately tattooed, so that as soon as required his head might pass as that of a distinguished rangatira. When the traffic in heads became general, the natives ceased altogether to preserve the heads of their friends, lest by any means they should fall into the hands of others and be sold. There were cases where slaves, rendered valuable with scrolls and curves and arabesques, effected their escape and carried their stolen value on their shoulders.

The Rev. J. G. Wood records the following incident: "One of my friends lately gave me a curious illustration of the trade in heads. His father wanted to purchase one, but did not approve of any that were brought for sale, on the ground that the tattoo was poor and not a good example of the skill of the native artists. The chief allowed the force of the argument, and pointing to a number of his people who had come on board, he turned to the intending purchaser saying, 'Choose which of these heads you like best, and when you come back I will take care to have it dried and ready for your acceptance.'"

The death duties seem to have taken curious forms in New Zealand, and to have been heavy. At every turn of the inquiry into this horrible subject, one is met with evidence of brutal cruelty, of low dishonesty, and of debasing greed. Maning quotes a case where the head of a living man was selected, sold and paid for beforehand, and duly delivered according to agreement; and he thinks it was no isolated case. At first the agents for the collection of these heads were ne'er-do-wells or deserters from ships who lived among the natives on the coast line; through them the skippers of trading or whaling vessels were accustomed to arrange for the "goods." But the trade began to grow in importance, and at length

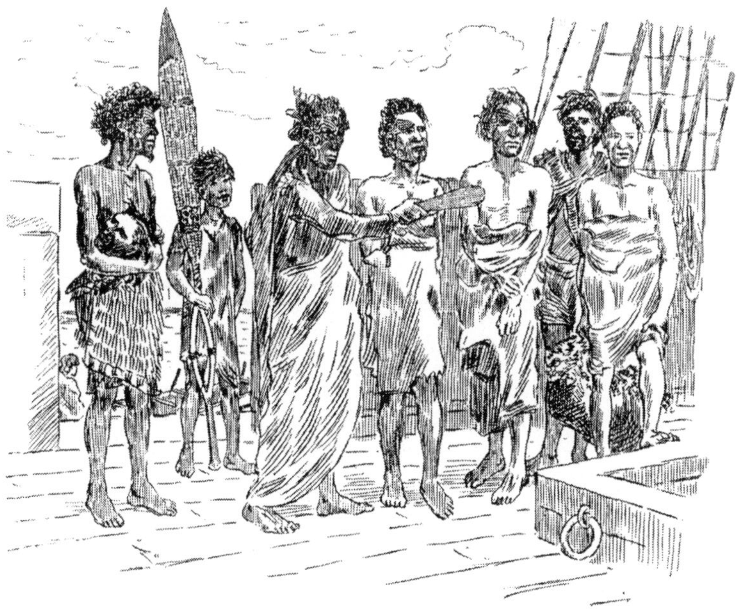

FIG. 152.—Offer of a living mokoed head for sale.
From a drawing by the Author.

agents were sent to select the best specimens, and "Baked Heads" acquired a separate entry among the imports at the Sydney Customs; and it was no uncommon thing to find them offered for sale in the streets of that city.

"Verax" writes in an old *Sydney Gazette*, "Passing through

George Street my attention was arrested by a very extraordinary sort of bundle under the arm of a man who was passing me on the footpath. I called to ask him what the bundle contained, when I beheld on his opening the covering a human head with long black

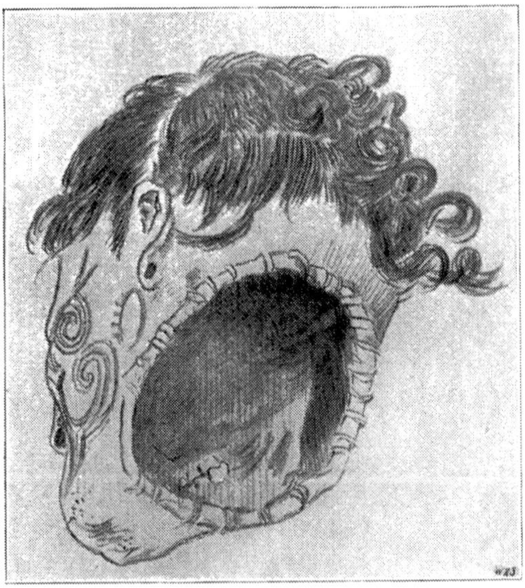

FIG. 153.—Opening at the neck showing a hoop and sewing of flax.
(*In Author's collection.*)

hair, in a state of perfect preservation. I asked the man if what he showed me was really a human head, when the man replied that it was the head of a New Zealander, which he had purchased from a person lately arrived from that country, and that he was going to dispose of it for two guineas to a gentleman who was about to embark for England."

The traffic still increased, and as the quality deteriorated, the dealers became dissatisfied, and some of them who went personally to examine and select living slaves whose heads they were willing to buy, were overtaken by a fate that deserves little pity.

Just before Te Pehi, mentioned in Part I., was killed, he was making free with a block of greenstone. The owner objected; and what followed is narrated by the Rev. James W. Stack in *Kaipohia*: "Te Pehi, who was now within four or five paces of the gate, turned and faced the speaker, and in the most contemptuous terms derided him for daring to question the actions of one so much his superior. 'Badly tattooed, badly tattooed,' he cried; 'what use would your ugly head be to me if I was to carry it with me to Kapiti; it would be worth nothing towards the purchase of a musket. But here is a man,' turning towards Te Panihi, who stood near him with a well-tattooed face, 'his head would be worth having; but you, with a valueless head, how dare you call in question the doings of Pehi tu a te rangi?'"

Rutherford, in his account of the chief Pomaree, referring to the year 1820, or 1821, throws more light on the history of the traffic in these dried heads. Pomaree's importance must be estimated from the fact that he had with him five hundred men, and numerous war canoes. Pomaree showed Rutherford several heads of numerous enemies he had killed; and these were to be taken to the Bay of Islands, and there to be exchanged for arms and powder with the ships that touched there. Pomaree was a famous taxidermist of heads, and was himself finely tattooed and had marks on his upper lip.

Mr. Nicholas also describes Pomaree as a man "gifted with keen commercial instinct" and most desirous of doing business. He told

Mr. Marsden he was quite ready to go and shoot some people who had killed his son, if ammunition and guns were given him, and

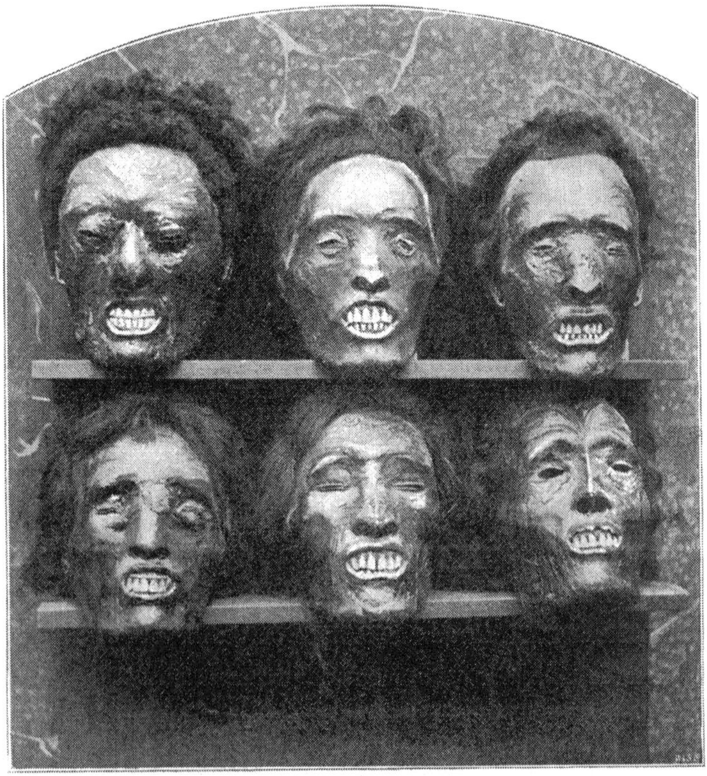

FIG. 154.—Group of heads in the Museum d'Histoire Naturelle, at Paris; one is a skin mounted on a plaster cast.

that he would then give an instance of his skill in preserving heads. Mr. Marsden told him never to mention again such shocking brutality, nor to bring any specimens of his inhumanity on the vessel Mr. Marsden was on board of. Mr. Nicholas says he fully believed that for the purposes of gain Pomaree would not hesitate to take the life of the first person he met, provided he could have done it with impunity.

I see in the *Missionary Register* for 1827 a letter from the Rev. H. Williams, recounting that a short time before Pomaree had fallen in battle, and with many of his men had been cut to pieces by a tribe which he had attacked.

The following well-known story from Maning's *Old New Zealand* illustrates the sordid nature of the traffic in heads on which I have been commenting. Maning recounts how he noticed a company of natives with finest cloaks and feathers on a little rising ground, and how he determined to introduce himself to them: "As I approached, one of these splendid individuals nodded to me in a very familiar sort of manner, and I, not to appear rude, returned the salute. I stepped into the circle formed by my new friends, and had just commenced a *Tena koutou*, when a breeze of wind came sighing along the hill-top. My friend nodded again,—his cloak blew to one side. What do I see?—or rather what do I not see? The head has no body under it! The heads had all been stuck on slender rods, a cross-stick tied on to represent the shoulders, and the cloaks thrown over all in such a natural manner as to deceive any one at a short distance, but a green pakeha, who was not expecting any such matter, to a certainty. I fell back a yard or two, so as to take a full view of this silent circle. I began to feel as if at last I had fallen into strange company. I began to look more closely at my companions, and to try to fancy what their character in life had been. One had undoubtedly been a warrior; there was something bold and defiant about the whole air of the head. Another was the head of a very old man, gray, shrivelled, and wrinkled. I was going on with my observations, when I was saluted by a voice from behind with : 'Looking at the 'eds, sir ?'

"It was one of the pakehas formerly mentioned.

"'Yes,' said I, turning round just the least thing quicker than ordinary.

"''Eds has been a getting scarce,' says he.

"'I should think so,' says I.

"'We an't 'ad a 'ed this long time,' says he.

"'The devil!' says I.

"'One o' them 'eds has been hurt bad,' says he.

"'I should think all were, rather so,' says I.

"'Oh no ; only one on 'em,' says he. 'The skull is split, and it won't fetch nothin',' says he.

"Oh, murder! I see, now,' says I.

"''Eds was werry scarce,' says he, shaking his own ''ed.'

"'Ah,' said I.

"They had to tattoo a slave a bit ago,' says he, 'and the villain ran away, tattooin' and all!' says he.

"'What!' said I.

"'Bolted afore he was fit to kill,' says he.

"'Stole off with his own head?' says I.

"'That's just it,' says he.

"'Capital felony!' says I.

"'You may say that, sir,' says he.

"'Good morning,' said I.

"I walked away, pretty smartly. 'Loose notions about heads in this country,' said I to myself; and involuntarily putting up my hand to my own, I thought somehow the bump of combativeness felt smaller, or indeed had vanished altogether. 'It's all very funny,' said I.

"All the heads on the hill were heads of enemies, and several of them are now in museums in Europe." "With reference to the knowing remarks of the pakeha who accosted me on the hill on the state of the head-market, I am bound to remark that my friend Mr. —— never speculated in this 'article,' but the skippers of many of the colonial trading schooners were always ready to deal with a man who had 'a really good head,' and used to commission such men as my companion of the morning to pick up heads for them."

It was a point of honour with the Maoris to try and save the heads of their tribe from the grasp of the enemy, who would sell them. Maning tells a story which illustrates this: "A small party of our friends had been surprised. Two brothers were flying for their lives down a hill side; a shot broke the leg of one of them and he fell; the enemy were close at hand; already the exulting cry of '*Na! na! mate rawa!*' was heard; the wounded man cried to the brother, 'Do not leave my head a plaything for the foe.' There was no time for deliberation. The brother did not deliberate; a few slashes with the tomahawk saved his brother's head, and he escaped with it in his hand, dried it, and brought it home."

Such are a few gruesome incidents of this truly awful traffic, which flourished so long.

Slowly but surely the traffic became a public scandal. The Maoris too had become possessed of all the arms they wanted, and discontinued a practice which was repulsive to their instincts and which they only adopted as a desperate measure to preserve their tribes from annihilation. In any case the practice was dying out. The credit of stopping it is due to Governor Darling of New South Wales. He was of course, it is said, exposed to very violent abuse, which continued for no inconsiderable time. Events, however, had occurred which brought public opinion to bear on a matter which, if it put a stop to a "gainful" traffic, was undoubtedly one that ought never to have reached the position it occupied in 1831. In January, 1831, Andrew Powers was one of the crew of a boat belonging to Joe Rowe, a trader in preserved heads at Kapiti. Amongst the heads which Joe Rowe had purchased were two of Taupo chiefs. These were seen at his store at Kapiti by their relatives who entreated him to give them up. He laughed at them. Finding he had arranged this expedition, they left before him and went to await his arrival. The boat, with Rowe and three white men, and a coloured man, entered the Wanganui River and they beached their boat to cook a meal. While eating, a party of natives joined company and one of the natives went and sat down in the boat. Rowe called out to Powers to turn him out, but knowing more of the natives, Rowe proceeded to do so himself, and the Maori promptly killed him with a blow on the head. Powers went to his help and was knocked overboard, but not killed. The rest of the party except the coloured man were killed. Rowe's head and that of another of the men were steeped and dried in the usual way for sale. One was too much chopped about to be worth preserving. The bodies of two were eaten. Powers was spared and lived with them, and was finally redeemed by the captain of a trading schooner for twenty-five pounds of tobacco. Powers, however, seeing only two preserved heads, inquired what had become of the third man, and was told that before being killed he had cried out for fear, and their *atuas* said the bodies of such as cried for fear of death were not to be eaten, lest those who eat should become cowards too. So he was buried in the sand. This account was given the Rev. Mr. Taylor in 1850 by Powers, who lived to a good old age.

In the same year as the Powers incident, another episode occurred which drew public attention to the matter. Jack, the master of a trading schooner, purchased in the Bay of Plenty the heads of some slain enemies who were from the Bay of Islands. Shortly after he and his schooner were at the Bay of Islands, where the heads were well known. A number of natives who came on board the vessel were shown the heads, and Jack poured them out of a sack on the ship's deck. The greatest commotion ensued, and such was the indignation aroused that Jack had to hasten away with his vessel, and was fired at soon after when met on the coast. Proceeding to Sydney, he disposed of his purchase, where the story excited the greatest interest. It was then that Governor Darling issued his Proclamation, which was justified by the enormity of the horrors involved in the trade. This document is worth transcribing. It runs thus :—

GOVERNMENT ORDER.

Colonial Secretary's Office,
Sydney, 16*th April*, 1831.

Whereas it has been represented to His Excellency the Governor that the masters and crews of vessels trading between this colony and New Zealand are in the practice (*sic*) of purchasing and bringing from thence human heads which are preserved in a manner peculiar to that country; and whereas there is strong reason to believe that such disgusting traffic tends greatly to increase the sacrifice of human life amongst savages whose disregard of it is notorious, His Excellency is desirous of evincing his entire disapprobation of the practice above mentioned as well as his determination to check it by all means in his power. And with this view His Excellency has been pleased to order that the Officers of the Customs do strictly watch and report every instance which they may discover of an attempt to import into this Colony any dried or preserved human heads in future, with the names of all parties concerned in any such attempt. His Excellency trusts that to put a total stop to this traffic it is necessary for him only thus to point out the almost certain and dreadful consequences which may be expected to ensue from a continuance of it, and the scandal and prejudice which it cannot fail to raise against the name and character of British traders in a country with which it has now become highly important for the merchants and traders of this colony, at least, to cultivate feelings of natural good-will. But if His Excellency should be disappointed of this reasonable expectation, he will feel it an imperative duty to take strong measures for totally suppressing the inhuman and very murderous traffic in question. His Excellency further trusts that all persons who have in their possession human heads recently brought from New Zealand, and particularly by the schooner *Prince of Denmark*, will immediately deliver them up for the purpose of being restored to the relations of the deceased parties to whom these heads belonged, this being the only possible reparation that can now be rendered, and application having been specially made to His Excellency for this purpose.

By His Excellency's command,

ALEXANDER MCLEAY.

In a subsequent issue of the *Gazette* the following notice appeared:

BAKED HEADS.

We have to state from authority that although the name of the *Prince of Denmark* is mentioned in Government Order No. 7, in consequence of a special application having being made to the Governor respecting the heads brought in that vessel, yet there is no reason whatever for supposing that the master and crew have been in any respect more blameable or more engaged in the traffic complained of than those of other vessels engaged in the New Zealand trade.

This humane and courageous effort to stop the abominations of the traffic in heads, was shortly followed by an Act which passed into law before New Zealand became a separate colony; and Governor Darling had the satisfaction of imposing a fine of £40 as well as publishing the names of those concerned. Public feeling ultimately supported the cause of humanity, and the trade faded away. It was only two years before (December, 1829) that the English Government in India formally abolished (through the agency of Lord William Bentinck) Suttee—the name given by writers to the custom of burning a widow on the funeral pyre of her husband. The practice was known in India when the Macedonians first touched in that country.

In 1838, when a United States expedition visited New Zealand, an effort was made to purchase some specimens of mokoed heads. Ultimately two were obtained from the steward of a missionary brig in the Bay of Islands; and Commodore Wilkes observes that this was about the last quarter in which he expected to find them. His remarks illustrate, however, the effects of Governor Darling's exertions. The law has never been formally repealed, although it provided that the possession of a dried head was punishable by fine. A few years ago this practically obsolete statute was used against Sir Julius Van Haast, curator of the Canterbury Museum, Christchurch. The museum contained a dried head which gave offence to some resident

Maories, who laid a complaint before the Governor, and the Attorney-General found that the old New South Wales ordinance was still in force, and the curator was officially informed that unless the offending exhibit was put out of sight, the law would be set in motion. The traffic discontinued in New Zealand has its feeble echo now among those who seek to possess preserved Maori heads.

CHAPTER XIII

MOKOED HEADS IN MUSEUMS AND COLLECTIONS

The time is approaching when the history of moko will be written only from the comments of previous writers and from the dried specimens of moko-mokai in the collections. With regard to literary sources of information, I think I have exhausted everything of interest, certainly most that is of importance in the preceding pages. As to the specimens in the museums and collections, I have travelled much and seen all I could. From many I have taken drawings, portraits, or photographs. Looking at the specimen heads, a lady might almost wonder if the object had had a sweetheart or a loving wife; while a man might speculate in what *mêlée* or ambuscade he fell, or whether friend, foe, or master used the tomahawk about his neck. The best specimens of moko-mokai in Europe are included in the list in my appendix; and I will now give some account of them.

The specimens range from 1770 to over 1830. So some of the earlier are perhaps as much as one hundred and twenty-five years old, though this is doubtful; the later are over sixty-five. The acquisition of the first specimen of moko-mokai by Europeans has already been noted. It was bought in the year 1770. The traffic

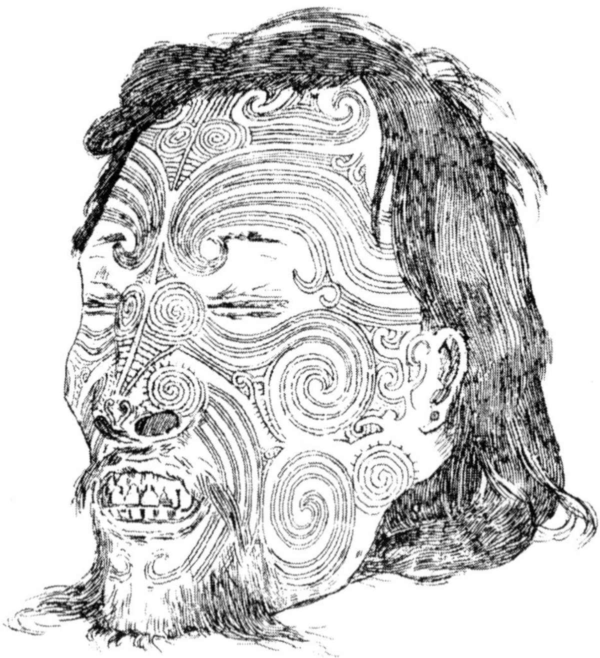

Fig. 155.—Royal College of Surgeons, London.

was, as we have lately seen, stopped as far as possible in 1831. Consequently, all the specimens now extant were obtained in the comparatively short period of about sixty years. It will however be found that a very large majority of dried heads were bought in the last twenty years of this period. For it was not until after 1820 that the traffic in them attained its wide dimensions and its revolting character. The majority then of the heads with which we have to deal are as moko-mokai from sixty-five to seventy-five years old. They are in fact in wonderful preservation. During 1864–66, and to any one interested, it could not be but a matter of regret that such fine heads as those that fell then should be buried. Many of them I sketched, and their moko is represented in these pages—the only memorial of them

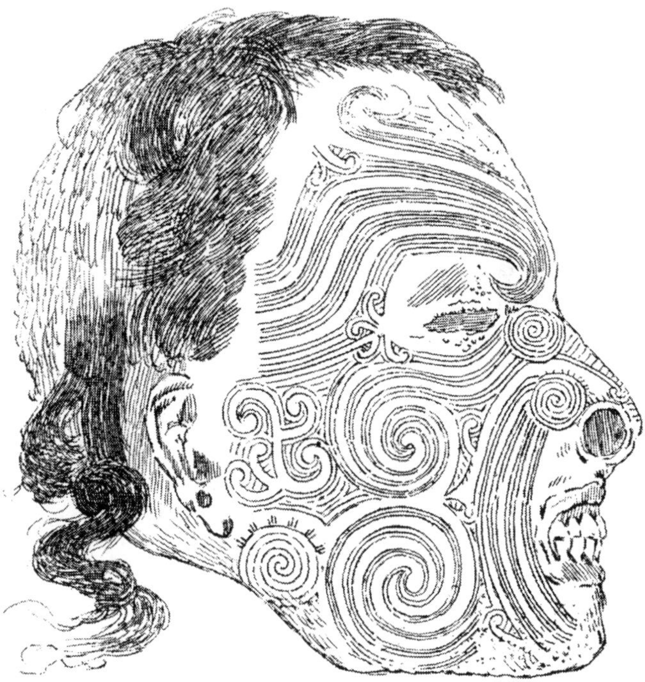

FIG. 156.—Royal College of Surgeons, London.

and their face-carving that now exists. The good head I spoke of just now "with eyes" is sketched on p. 145. On p. 162 there is a drawing of a boy's head tattooed after death (left eye gone). The hair of these heads is usually more firmly secured than

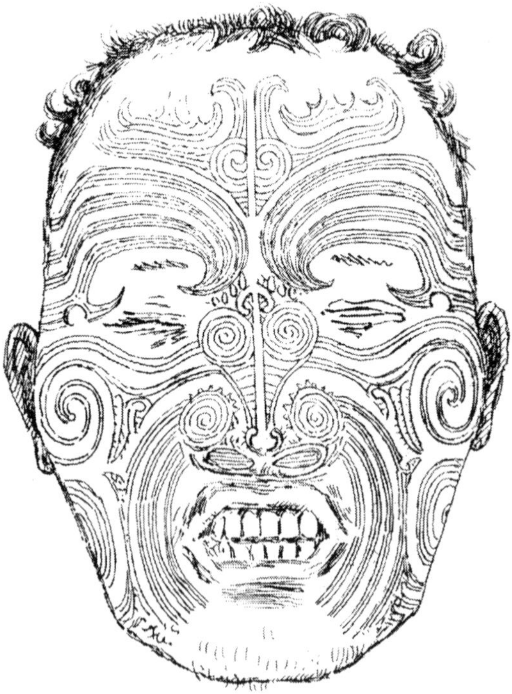

FIG. 157.—Specimen in the Royal College of Surgeons, London.
(Presented by the late Sir Erasmus Wilson.)

when their owners were alive; for owing to the careful drying after steaming and other precautions the hair of a dried head is nearly ineradicable; though it remains, as before, long, wild, and unkempt. In the case of chiefs, it was sometimes combed in a special fashion—the beard was scanty, a little moustache or tuft under the chin sometimes remains, and the eyebrows keep well. One well-whiskered head is in the Royal College of Surgeons; and it is represented on this page. All sorts of hair are included in the collected specimens, black and brown, straight and curly, matted and frizzled, and even gray and reddish. There is one very fair-haired specimen in the Florence

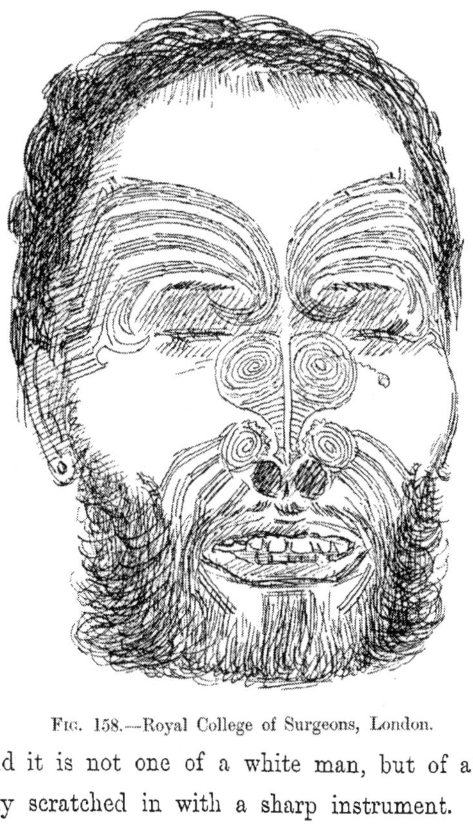

FIG. 158.—Royal College of Surgeons, London.

Museum, and it is not one of a white man, but of a native, the moko lightly scratched in with a sharp instrument. The Maori teeth, too, are always splendid; and in the dried head they remain like ivory. As already noted, in most faces the hair was quite eradicated and the flesh on the upper lip and chin

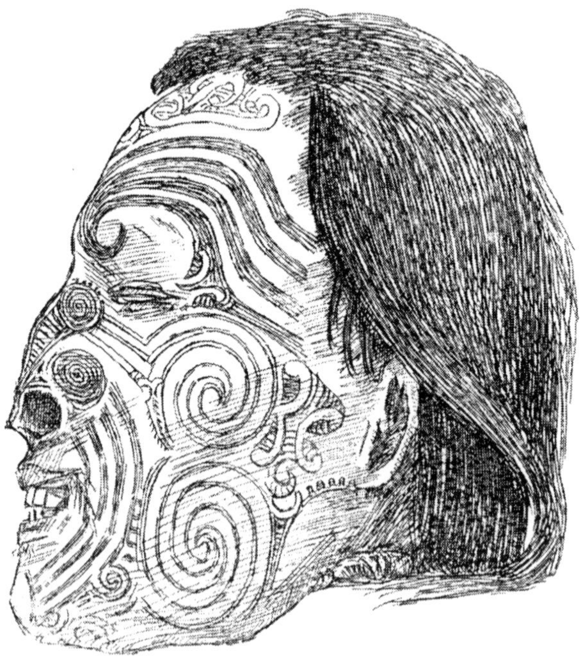

FIG. 159.—Head showing some *post-mortem* tattooing.
(*Royal College of Surgeons, London.*)

was often quite smooth. There are no stubbly chins amongst the old dried specimens. The clean dried state of these skulls can best be observed by turning over a specimen and observing the marks of the smoke in the interior. In the instance given at p. 172 the opening large enough for the hand will be remarked. It is increased by the removal of the base of the skull. The hoop binding of the base is neat. Sometimes a flax loop is added so that the head can be hung in a certain position.

Post-mortem moko is easily distinguished by the non-appearance of the subcutaneous colour; and where moko was incomplete at the time of death the pattern was often added to. But the difference of the cuts on the live and on the hardened flesh is

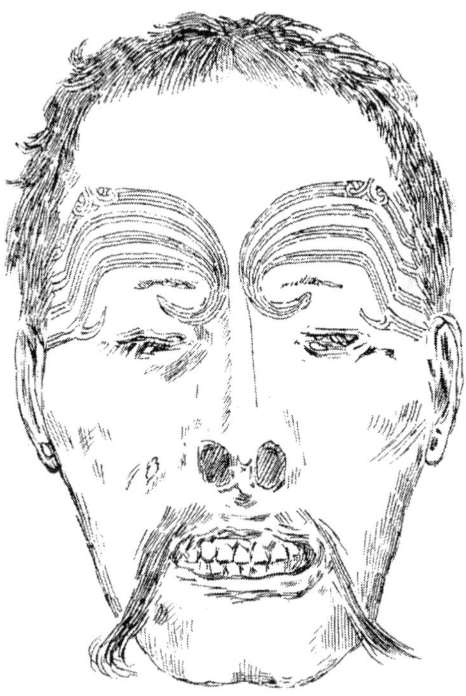

FIG. 160.—Royal College of Surgeons, London.

easily recognised. Again, sometimes the pattern scored in life has been recut deeper into the leathery surface after death. These new marks on the old lines are also readily distinguished. In one of the British Museum specimens this *post-mortem* tracing is of totally different pattern to that cut during life, and this is the

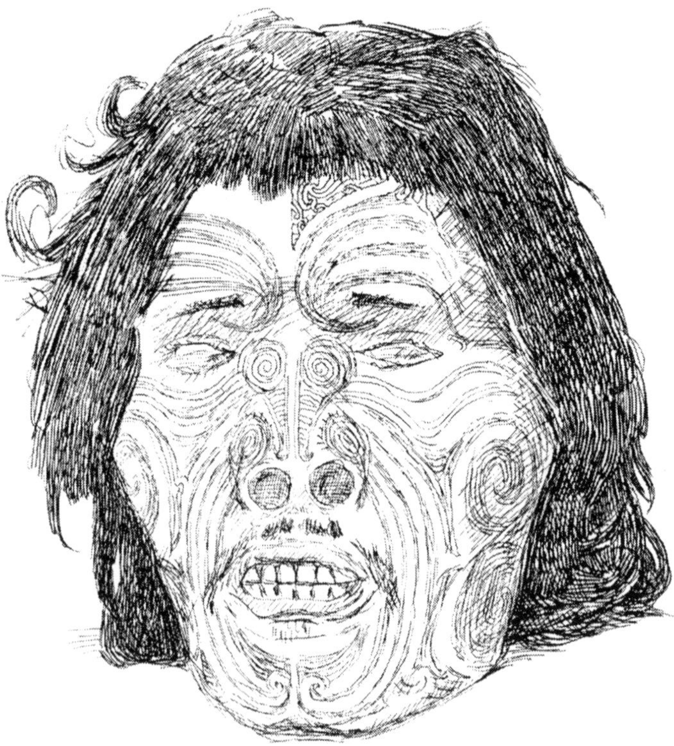

FIG. 161.—Specimen in British Museum. The best in that collection.

more regrettable as the original pattern was not only good and complete and well preserved, but the new one is carelessly worked or scratched, and looks pale over the blue of the older and real moko. In some heads in collections the effects of careless curatorship are readily seen—damp and over-varnish being the chief causes; while there are many as trim, neat, and fresh as when first dried and smoked.

Where the eyes are preserved, it is usually concluded that the head was dried tenderly by relations or friends, or at special order. The open mouth with the lips stretched wide is frequent in the collections, and mostly indicates an enemy's head; while sewn-up lips or a pouting mouth indicate (as elsewhere stated) a friend's embalming. These last are of course rarer. The

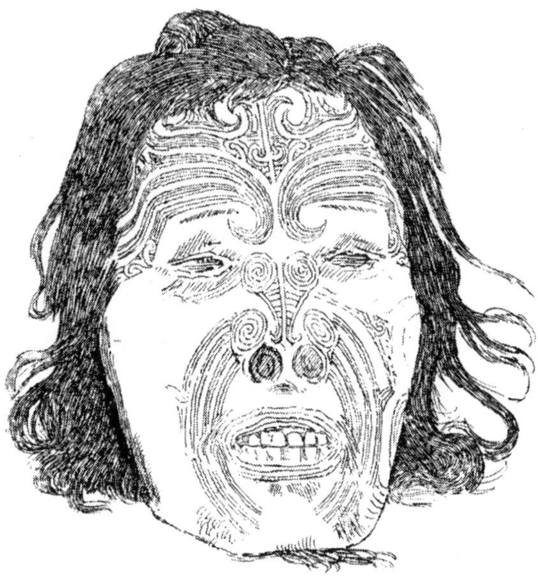

FIG. 162.—Specimen in British Museum. The lips have been cut after death.

noses are plugged up, and a stick is used to preserve the shape; and there are instances of over- or too little stuffing. The contraction of the skin makes the nose appear shorter, affects the lips, and draws down the centre of the forehead. The ears are always shrivelled up, and the lobe pierced to carry a pendent

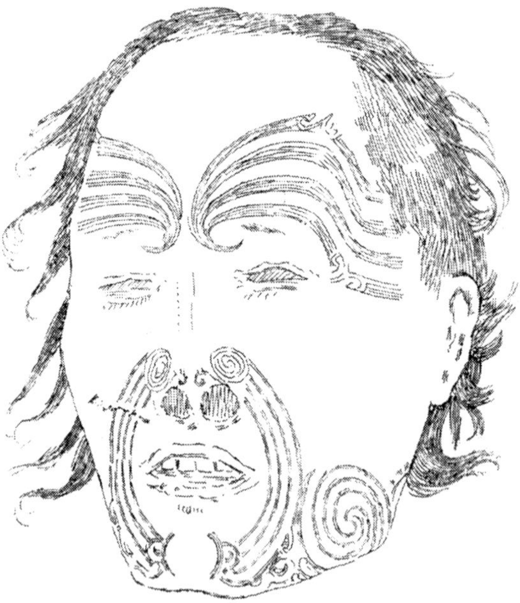

FIG. 163.—Specimen in British Museum.

ornament. The skin of the cheeks is always tightly stretched. One specimen at Berlin has some of the neck-skin attached. In some museums one finds the dried skin of the face hanging over a skull, or even over a plaster cast; there is an instance of the former at the Royal College of Surgeons, and of the latter in the Natural History Museum in Paris. The colour of the skin varies much, and is dependent on that of the skin in life, and on the manner of curing and on the care employed in keeping.

These dried Maori heads, even those which have only very few lines of moko, and also the occasional specimens of dried European heads, are now valuable. The head is a work of art; and its value is subject to all the vicissitudes that affect the value of other works of art. They are all very scarce; and the number in private hands

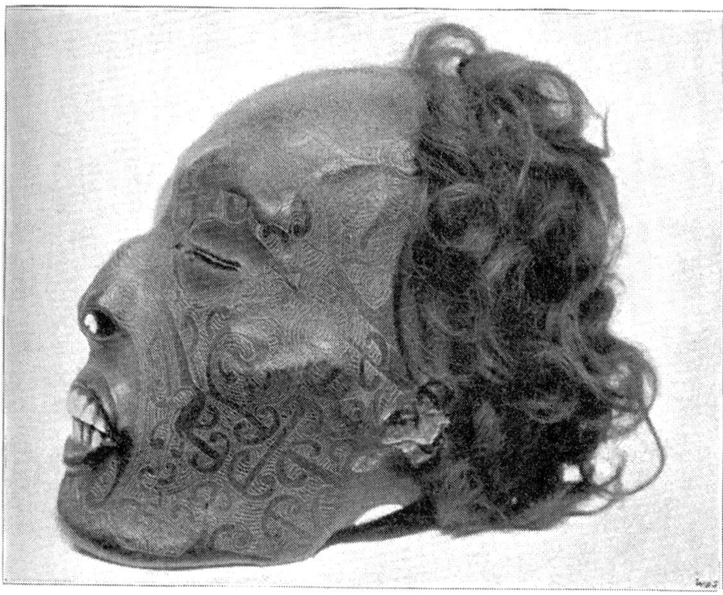

FIG. 164.—Specimen in British Museum. The good and complete moko done during life has been nearly covered all over with *post-mortem* carving of quite a different design.

(as distinct from museum ownership) is very few; while only those in private hands can ever be sold. The early want of appreciation of these mokoed heads as works of art also affects their ownership. It is curious that the museums in New Zealand and Sidney have the fewest and worst.

The two heads in the Auckland (New Zealand) Museum once formed part of the collection of Dr. Barnett Davis, of London. I

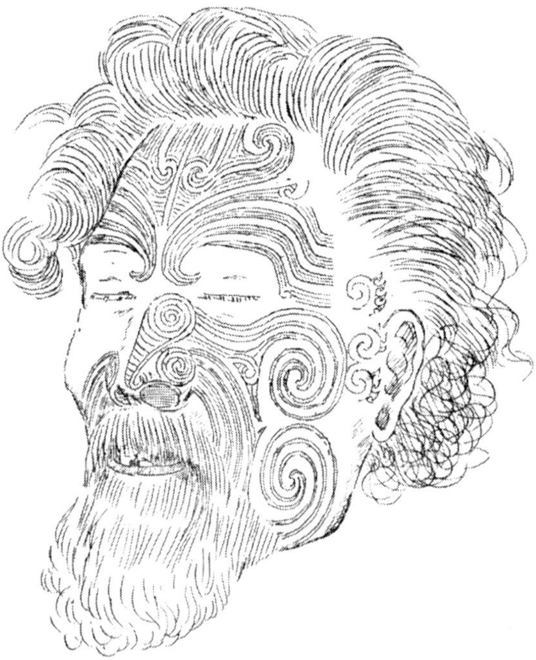

FIG. 165.—Specimen in Author's collection.

give pictures of one. Dr. B. Davis's collection was sold about 1880, and these specimens were acquired from the purchaser in exchange for a pair of Moriori crania from the Chatham Islands. When the mokoed heads reached Auckland they were recognised by some natives from the Bay of Islands, as two of Hawiti's tribe, named

Moetarau and Koukou. These persons were killed in a fight which took place about sixty years earlier, near the present railway station

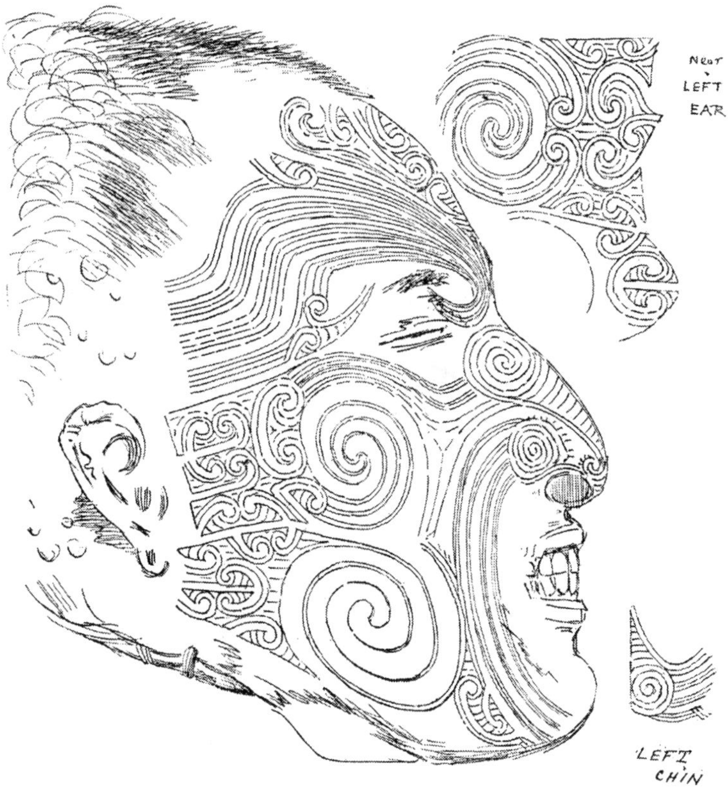

Fig. 166.—Specimen in St. George's Hospital, London. Some of the work very good.

of Opua. They were taken to Te Puna, where they were preserved by an old chief named Muru Paenga, and were afterwards presented to the party of Hokianga natives who had assisted in the fight.

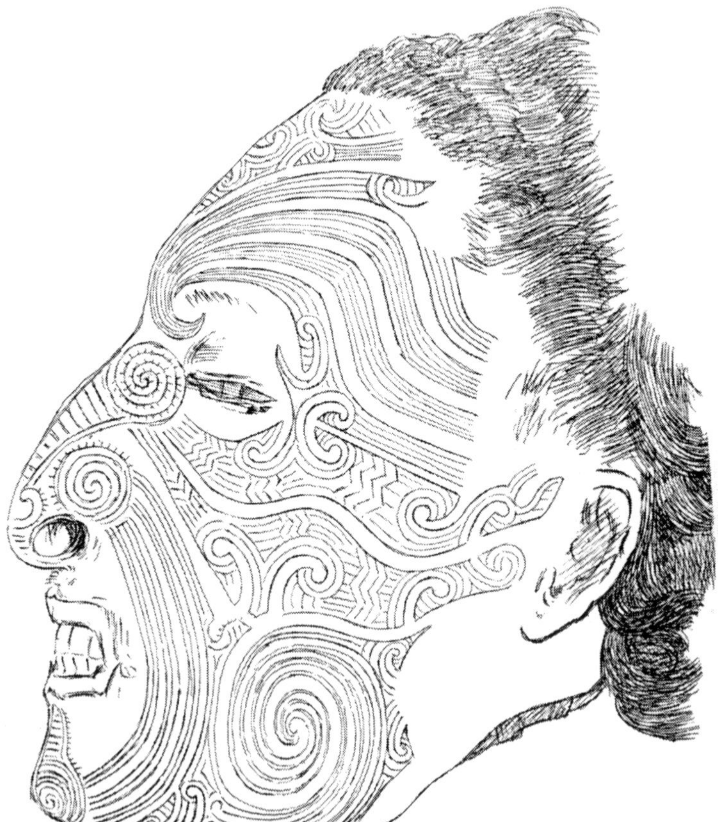

Fig. 167.—Specimen in Museum at Halifax, Yorks; showing bands of tattooing on cheek: a very good specimen of the finest moko.

By these last the two heads were sold to the captain of a vessel for £20. They were among the last heads preserved in the Bay of Islands.

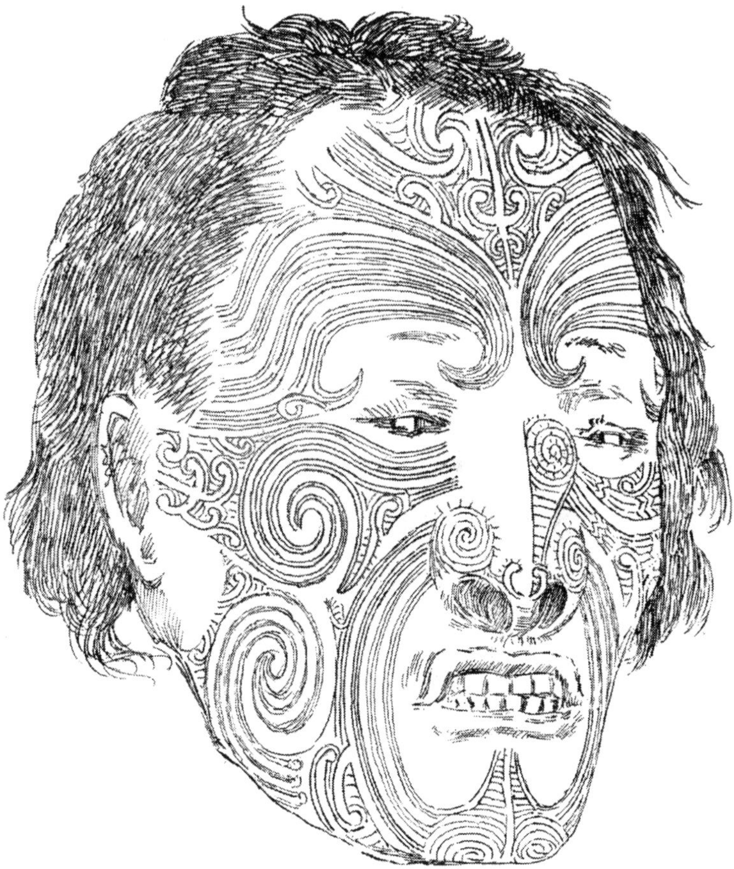

FIG. 168.—Same specimen in Halifax Museum; showing unfinished nose. Varying patterns.

I will give a list, with remarks, of some well-preserved specimens.

At the Royal College of Surgeons there are six heads and a

skin. At Aberdeen Marischal College there are seven. At South Kensington Museum there is one. At the British Museum there are four heads; and at St. George's Hospital one. At Guy's Hospital

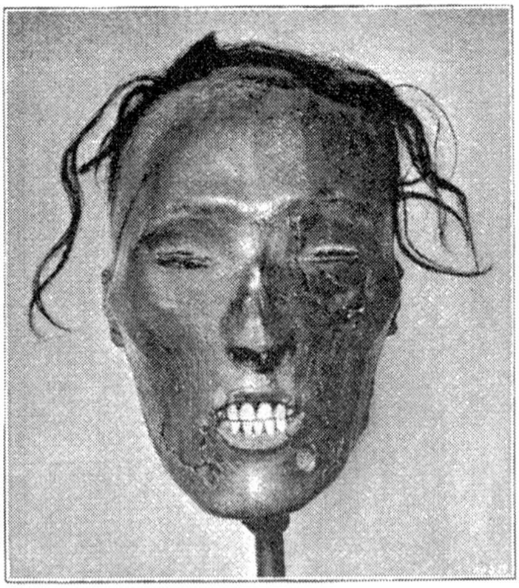

Fig. 169.—Specimen in Berlin Museum of Ethnology.

two, and a good wax model from nature of the Maori patient who died in the hospital in 1849. The impression in wax of his tattooed face has come out very well. His moko was deep coarse work,—a really good specimen of a man partly tattooed. The furrows are well shown in the model. His marks may be thus described: Part of set of radial lines on forehead; one, right nostril and right tip of nose; two cheek lines right and left; left upper and right lower lips with four lines; chin rather well done. At King's College Museum there are two and an infant's.

At the Paris Muséum d'Histoire Naturelle there are six heads obtained in the course of voyages by Buchanan de Freycinet, de Lesson and Maxime du Camp, and of these one is a skin mounted on a plaster cast. At Plymouth there are four. At Berlin, Königliches Museum für Völkerkunde, there are two, one fitted with glass eyes. At Auckland (New Zealand) there are two specimens, the story of which has been told. At Christchurch (New Zealand),

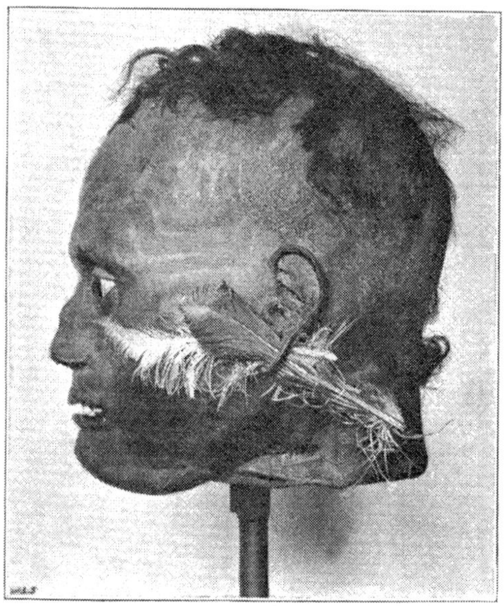

FIG. 170.—Specimen in Berlin Museum of Ethnology.

Canterbury Museum, there are two—of which one is from the Cambridge Museum and bears their number 1013, and one taken from Taranaki to England in 1837. At the Sydney Australian

Museum there are two not very good specimens. At the Florence Anthropological Museum there are two, one of which has light

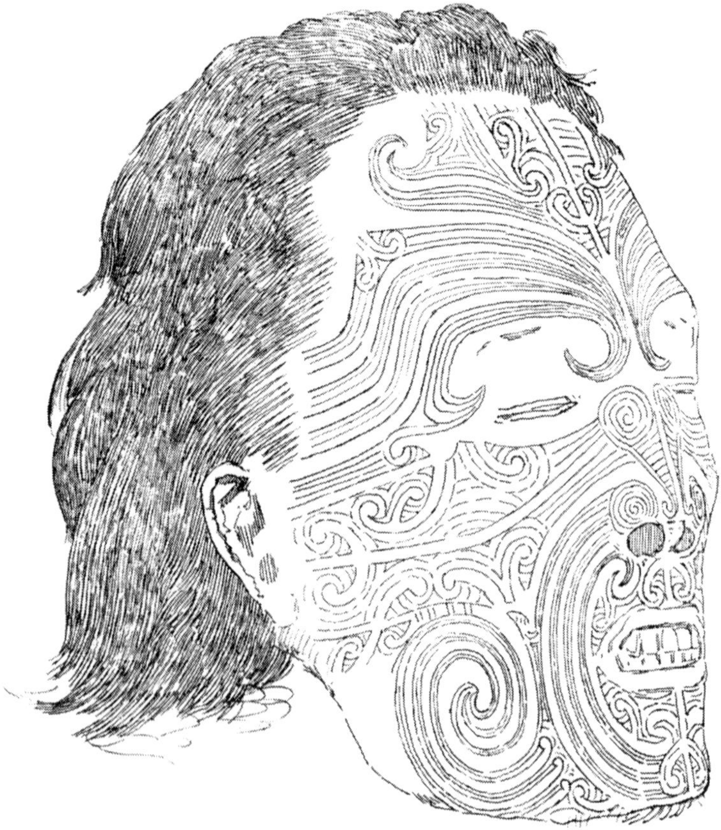

FIG. 171.—Specimen in South Kensington Museum, London. Mostly *post-mortem* moko.

hair. At the Washington Smithsonian Institution there is one specimen, and at the Army Medical Museum there are two bought from a missionary ship by Commodore Wilkes in 1838. These heads are finely mokoed. At Halifax (Yorkshire) there is one, evidently done with iron tools. At Devizes (Wilts) in the museum of the Archæological and Natural History Society there is one. At the Exeter Albert Memorial Museum there is one. At the Whitby

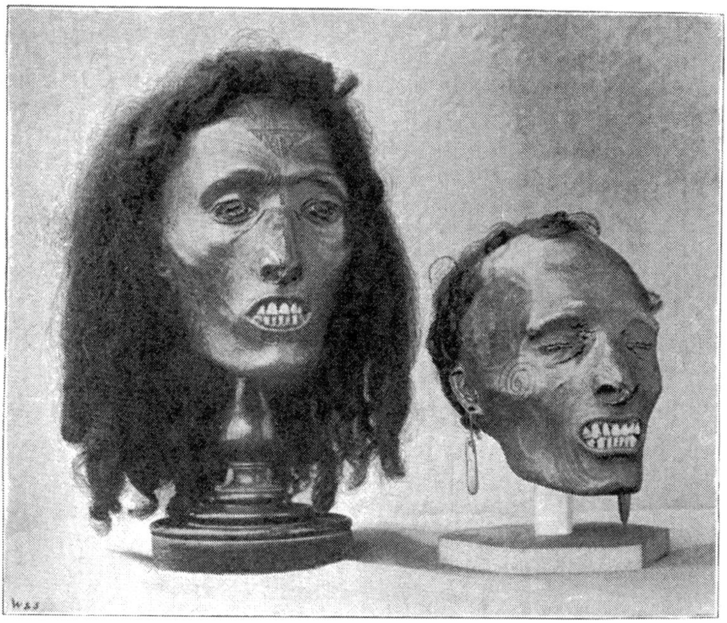

FIG. 172.—Baron Von Hügel's collection in the Museum of Archæology and Ethnology, Cambridge.

Museum there are three. At Hull, in the Royal Institution, there are two. At Sheffield there is one specimen. At Saffron Walden there are three, including one of a woman. In Rome, at the

Anthropological Museum, there is one. At York and Dover Museums there are one each. At Oxford, at the University

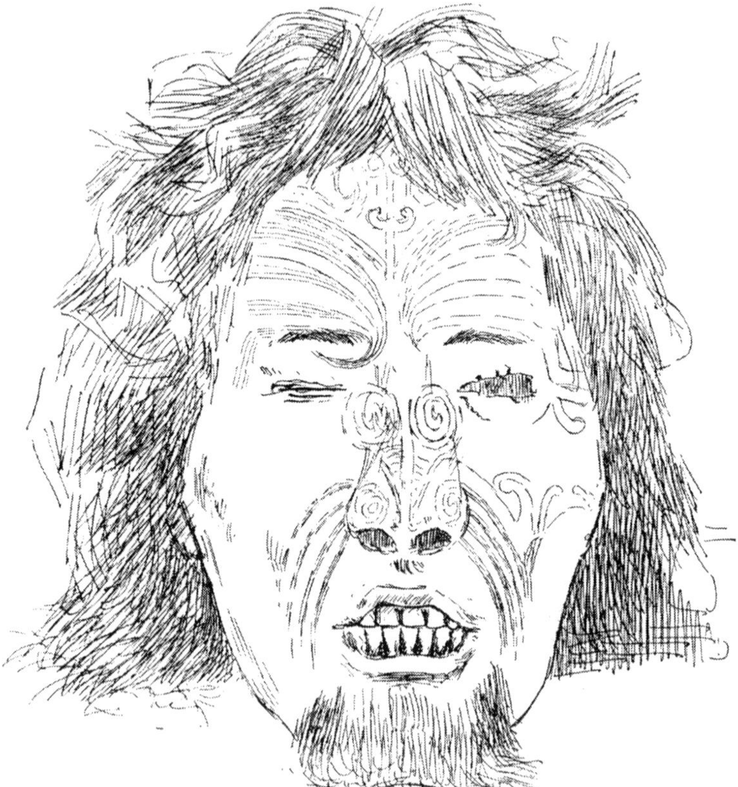

FIG. 173.—Specimen in Ethnological Museum at Florence. Pattern scratched in as an outline, preparatory to tattooing.

Museum, there are four; and at Cambridge (Baron von Hügel) there are two. At Dublin there are several—namely, at the Science and Art Museum two specimens, at Trinity College three,

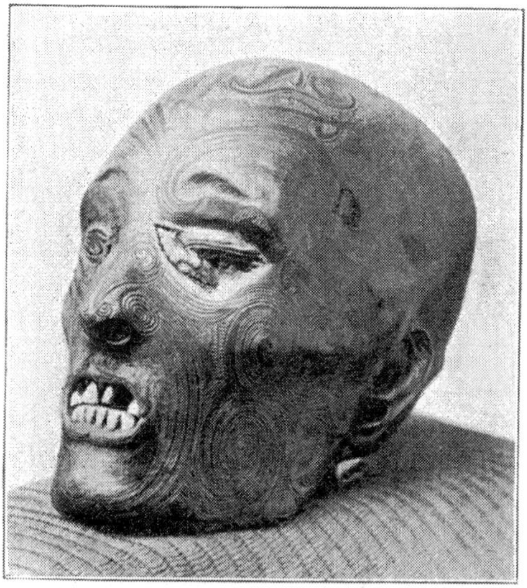

FIG. 174.—Specimen in Auckland Museum, N.Z.

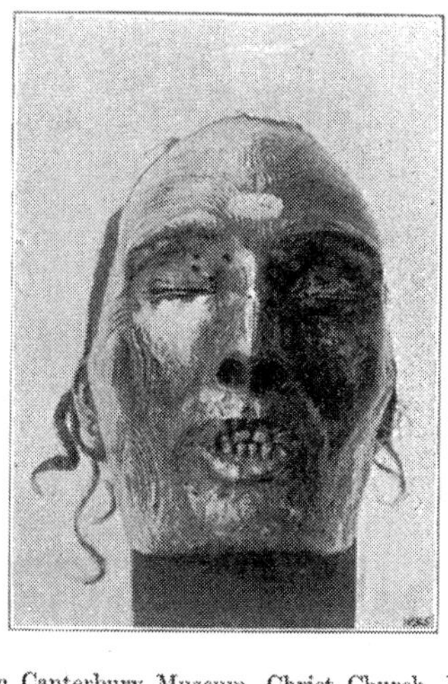

FIG. 175.—Specimen in Canterbury Museum, Christ Church, N.Z., said to have been sent to England from Taranaki in 1837.

and at the Royal College of Surgeons four. The Museum of University College, London, has two, one being among the best in existence. At Copenhagen, at the National Museum, there is one. At Munich,

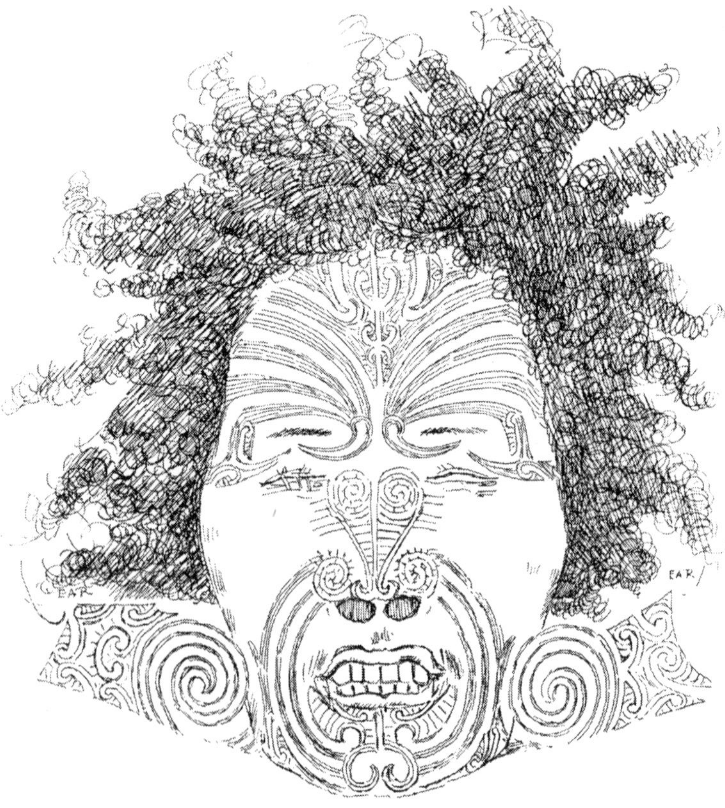

FIG. 176.—Specimen in the Ethnological Museum at Florence. Six lines only from nostrils to chin.

at the Ethnographical Museum, there is one brought from London; and Professor Gabriel Max has a collection, I am informed. Others will be found at Bremen (1), Göttingen (1), Hamburg (1), Moscow (1). Professor H. Giglioli at Florence has one. Mr. J. W. Colmer has one of a boy; and the author has a collection

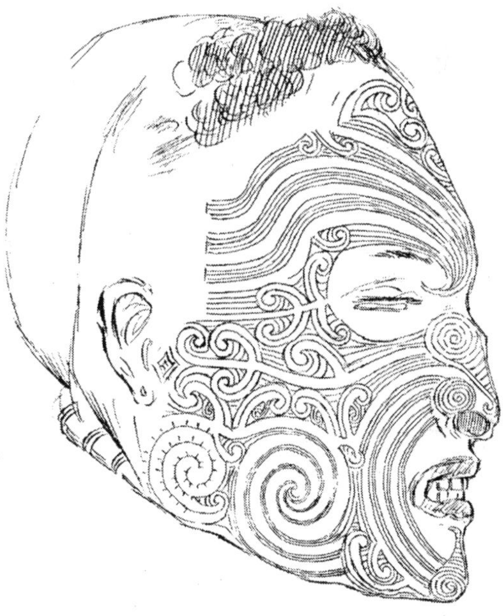

FIG. 177.—Head in Oxford University Museum, the other side has spiral on the cheek.

and also a thigh and many drawings of Maoris who were in or fell in the fighting, 1864–6.

Many of these specimens are represented in this book by drawings which I have made, as photography does not give their blue lines well, nor the markings on skins. This art of a bygone day and these pictures of Maori faces have long been my study.

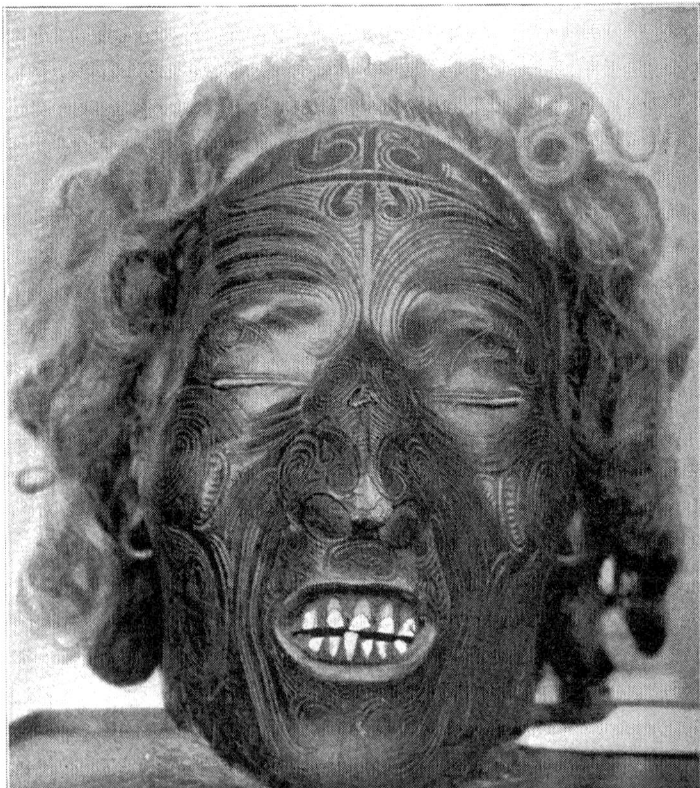

FIG. 178.—Specimen in Göttingen Museum; showing large amount of *post-mortem* work.

Whether a thought will be bestowed on them by others I cannot say. But for those who are interested I have sought to collect everything that is worth recording; omitting much, no doubt,

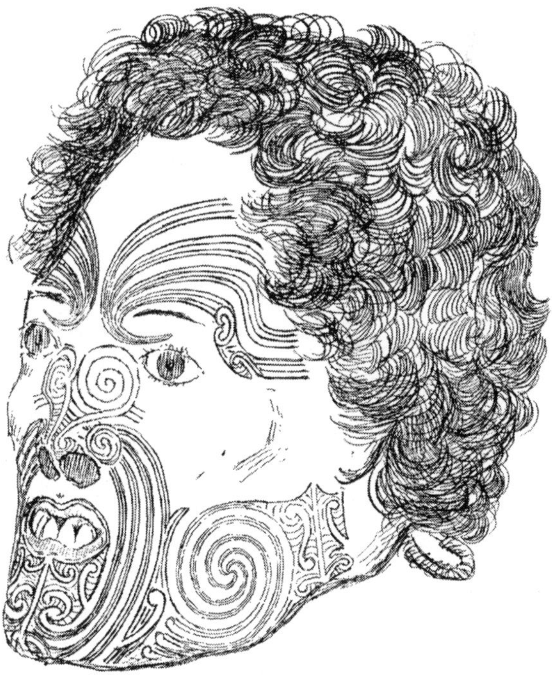

FIG. 179.—Specimen owned by Professor H. Giglioli, of Florence, glass eyes added by a European taxidermist. Moko very bold.

but omitting only where I doubt authenticity. Should my book be considered "whai mana" or a "standard work" on this particular element in Maori life and history I shall be more than satisfied. I can only, in my concluding words, repeat what I have said in my preface—namely, that it has been my object to record what I can of a subject that must one day pass out of remembrance. A full description of Maori art life has yet to be written; and even this little book in no way exhausts that portion of it that is dealt with.

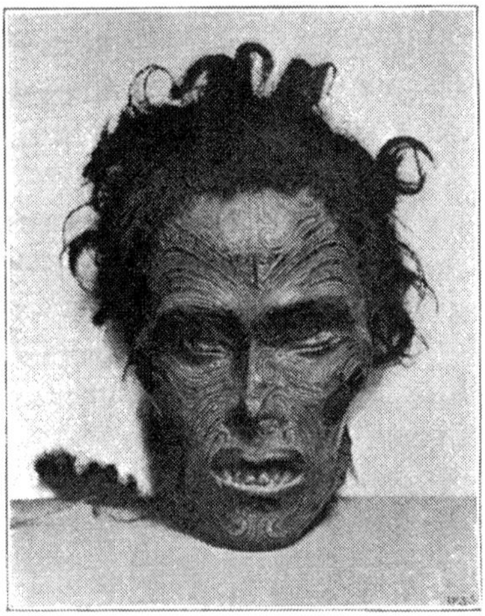

FIG. 180.—Head in Plymouth Museum.
(*From a photograph.*)

AUTHORITIES CONSULTED

ANGAS, G. F. *The New Zealanders Illustrated.* London, 1847.

„ „ *Polynesia.* London, 1866.

ANOUTCHINE, Professor D. N., of Moscow, President of the Imperial Society for Natural Science. *Anthropology and Ethnography.*

ANTHROPOLOGICAL SOCIETY of London.

BALFOUR, Henry, M.A., Esq., University Museum of Oxford.

BIDWILL, J. C., Esq. *Rambles in New Zealand.* 1839.

BOOSÉ, J. R., Esq., Librarian, Royal Colonial Institute.

BROWN, Alex., Esq., Marischal College, Aberdeen.

BROWN, R., Dr. *The Races of Mankind.* London, 1875.

BROWN, W., Esq. *New Zealand and its Aborigines.* London, 1845.

BROWNE, C. R., Esq., M.D., Anthropological Laboratory, Trinity College, Dublin.

BROWNE, Montagu, Esq., F.G.S., &c., Leicester.

BRUTTON, E., Major.

BUCHNER, Dr. M., Munich.

BULLER, Rev. James. *New Zealand Past and Present.* London, 1880.

BULLER, Sir Walter, K.C.M.G., F.R.S.

BURTON, John, Esq., Falmouth.

CAPTAIN JAMES COOK'S *Voyages.*

CASARTELLI, Rev. L. C., Manchester.

Church Missionary Registers.

CLARKE, C. M., Lt.-General, C.B.

COLENSO, W., Esq. *On a Better Knowledge of the Maori Race.* "Transactions of the New Zealand Institute." Wellington, 1881.

COLMER, J. W., Esq.

COOTE, C. H., British Museum.

CRAIK, G. L. *The New Zealander's Library of Entertaining Knowledge.* London, 1824.

CROZET. *Nouveau Voyage à la Mer du Sud.* Paris, 1783.

CRUISE, R. A., Major in 84th Regiment. *Journal of a Ten Months' Residence in New Zealand.*

CUTTER, Miss E.

DALLAS, J., Esq., Exeter Albert Memorial Museum.

DANGERFIELD, H. E., Esq.

DARWIN, C.

DENTON, Geo., Esq., Wellington, New Zealand.

DIEFFENBACH, Ernest *Travels in New Zealand by Routes through the Interior.*

DILLON, Captain P.

DOLAN, Thos., Esq. M.D.

DOUBLEDAY, G. A., Esq., Anthropological Society.

DUMONT, D'Urville. *Voyage au Pôle Sud.* Paris, 1834.

EARLE, Augustus. *Narrative of a Residence in New Zealand.* London, 1832.

EDGE-PARTINGTON, J., Esq.

EDWARDS, Milne A., Natural History Museum, Paris.

EDWARDS, S., Esq.. Royal Colonial Institute.

ELLIS, W., Polynesian Researches. London, 1829.

ETHERIDGE, R., Esq., Australian Museum, Sydney.

FENTON, W. H., Esq.

FITZROY, Captain.

FOWLER, Miss.

FRANK, G. A., Esq.

FRANKS, Sir Augustus Wollaston, K.C.B.

GIGLIOLI, Professor H. H., Florence.

GOODE, G. Brown, Esq., Assistant Secretary, Smithsonian Institution, Washington, U.S.A.

Graphic, The.

GREY, Sir George, P.C., K.C.B., F.R.S., &c.

HAMILTON, A., Esq., Registrar of the University of Otago.

HAWKESWORTH, J. *Voyages in the Southern Hemisphere.* London, 1773.

HOCHSTETTER, Baron Ferdinand von.

HOCKEN, Dr. T. M., F.L.S.

HORNIMAN, F. John, Esq., M.P., F.R.G.S., F.Z.S., &c.

HUDSON, S. P., Esq., Hull.

HÜGEL, Baron von, Archæological Museum, Cambridge.

HUTCHINSON, Jonathan, Esq., F.R.S., LL.D.

HUTTON, F. W., Canterbury Museum, Christchurch.

KENNAWAY, Walter, Esq., New Zealand Government.

KENNAWAY, L. J., Esq.

KERRY, Nicholls J., Esq., F.R.G.S. *The Origin, Physical Characteristics, Manners, and Customs of the Maori Race.* ("The Journal of the Anthropological Institute of Great Britain and Ireland." Vol. 15.)

KING, W., Esq.

LANGLEY, S. P., Smithsonian Institution.

LAWRENCE, T. W. P., Esq., M.B., F.R.C.S.

LEDYARD, John. *Journal of Captain Cook's Last Voyages*, 1783. Hartford, Conn.

LEE, J. B., Esq.

LUBBOCK, Sir John, Bart., &c.

LUCAS, F. W., Esq.

MANING, F. E. *Old New Zealand, by a Pakeha Maori.* London, 1863.

MANTEGAZZA, Professor. The Senator, Florence.

MARGOLIOUTH, C. L., Esq.

MARSHALL, W. Barrett, Surgeon R.N. *Second Visit to New Zealand.*

MEDLICOTT, H. E., Esq., Secretary, Wiltshire Archæological Society.

MERKEL, Fr., Professor, Göttingen.

MEYER, H., Professor, Leipsic.

MIDDLEBROOK, T. G., Esq.

MUNDY, Colonel J. *Our Antipodes.* 1847.

NICHOLAS, J. L. *Narrative of a Voyage to New Zealand.* London, 1817.

OBST, Dr., Director Leipsic Museum.

O'DELL, Stackpool, Esq.

OPPENHEIM, Anne, Professor.

PARKER, J. W., Esq. *British Colonisation of New Zealand.* 1837.

PARKINSON, Sydney. *Journal.* London, 1773.

PIGORINI, Professor, Rome.

PLAYFAIR, H., Esq., M.D., King's College, London.

POLACK, J. S., Esq. *Manners and Customs of the New Zealanders.* London, 1840.

POOLE, Mrs. C. G.

QUICK, R., Esq., F.J.A., Curator, Horniman Museum.

RADLOFF, Dr., St. Petersburg.

READ, Hercules, Esq., F.S.A.

REGÀLIA, E., Assistant Curator, Anthropological Museum, Florence.

RIENZI, G. L. Domeny. *Italian Edition.* Venice, 1843.

RUSSELL, Purvis, Esq.

SAINTSBURY, Mrs.

SAVAGE, John, Surgeon. *Account of New Zealand.* Edinburgh, 1807.

SCHAUNSLAND, Professor, Bremen.

SCHERZER, Dr. Karl. *Novara Expedition,* 1857–8–9.

SCOTT, J. Alfred, Esq., M.D.

SHAW, L. E., Dr.

SHERRINS, R. A. A. *Early History of New Zealand to* 1840.

STACK, Rev. J. W.

STEWART, Professor Charles, Royal College of Surgeons.

STONEHOUSE, Wm., Esq., Literary and Philosophical Society, Whitby.

TAYLOR, Rev. Rich., M.A., F.G.S. *Te ika a Maui.* 1870.

THANE, G. D., Professor.

THOMSON, A. S., M.D. *The Story of New Zealand.* London, 1851.

TREGEAR, E., Esq., F.R.G.S.

UMLAUFF, J. F., Esq., Hamburg.

VALLANCE, David, Esq., Edinburgh.

VON LUSCHAN, Professor, Berlin.

WADE, W. R., Esq. *A Journey in the Northern Island.* Hobart Town, 1842.

WAKEFIELD, E. J., Esq. *Adventure in New Zealand,* 1839–44.

WALLACE, A. R., Esq.

WALSH, Rev. Phillip.

WEBSTER, W. D., Esq.

WELLCOME, Henry S., Esq.

WHITE, J., Esq. *The Ancient History of the Maori: His Mythology and Traditions.*

WILKES, Charles, Commander, U.S. Navy. *Voyage round the World.*

WORTH, N., Esq., Plymouth.

YATE, Rev. William. *Account of New Zealand, and of the Church Missionary Society's Mission in the Northern Island.* London, 1835.

YOUNG, R., Esq. *The Southern World.* London, 1858.

INDEX

INDEX

2083564R00130

Printed in Great Britain
by Amazon.co.uk, Ltd.,
Marston Gate.